Self-Analysis for Analysts

of related interest

Thought
From the Skin Ego to the Thinking Ego
Didier Anzieu
ISBN 1 85302 401 5

Group
Claudio Neri
Translated by Christine Trollope
ISBN 1 85302 416 3

Circular Reflections
Selected Papers of Malcolm Pines
Malcolm Pines
Foreword by Saul Scheidlinger
ISBN 1 85302 492 9 pb
ISBN 1 85302 493 7 hb

Self-Analysis for Analysts

Karl König

Jessica Kingsley Publishers
London and Bristol, Pennsylvania

First published in the United Kingdom in 1997 by
Jessica Kingsley Publishers Ltd
116 Pentonville Road
London N1 9JB, England
and
1900 Frost Road, Suite 101
Bristol, PA 19007, U S A

Library of Congress Cataloging in Publication Data

A CIP catalogue record for this book is available from the Library of Congress

British Library Cataloguing in Publication Data

A CIP catalogue record for this book is available from the British Library

ISBN 1-85302-476-7

Printed and Bound in Great Britain by
Athenaeum Press, Gateshead, Tyne and Wear

Contents

Preface

Practically all psychoanalysts and many analytically oriented psycho-therapists take it as a matter of course that analysis or participation in a psychoanalytic experiential group should be followed by self-analysis. This applies to patients, and even more so to analysts. Freud (1937) wrote about analysis being interminable. The capacity to analyse oneself is useful in private life and necessary in countertransference analysis. Anybody who has ever experienced how his internal conflicts are actualized in the bipersonal field of analysis and the intensity of feelings which then occurred and who has also experienced the power of an analyst's interpretations that gave structure to what was experienced and helped to understand it, might think that self-analysis cannot be anything but insufficient.

However, in every analysis there are phases of working-through. The analysand uses insights derived from his relationship to the analyst in understanding his relationships with other persons. Many wishes and fears occur first in relationships with other persons, not in the relationship with the therapist, and only later become manifest in the bipersonal psychoanalytic field. Also, in every analysis there are phases when analysand and analyst both look at the analysand's relationships with other persons. The analyst is then in the role of an expert. Transferences directed on him are still present, but often less intense.

Self-analysis could be compared to these phases of analysis. In self-analysis, the analyst is not present, but he can be remembered. He has previously shown the analysand how to work in analysis. The analysand now uses on his own what he has learned. On the other hand, no person with a more objective way of looking at things is now present. Of course, the analyst can never be quite objective, but he can be more so than the analysand himself because he is not as directly involved in the analysand's relationships. Also, analysand and analyst do not share the same blind spots. The analyst will probably not miss the same things his analysand does. It is often taken as a matter of course that the analyst has fewer blind spots than the analysand, but this is not even necessary. Quite often it is sufficient that the blind spots are not the same.

Working with an analyst has other advantages. The asymmetry in the analysand–analyst relationship – which, among other things, shows in different roles: the role of the analysand and the role of the analyst – facilitates the emergence of certain transferences which frequently remain latent in daily life. Sometimes, self-analysis is restricted to finding new applications for what the self-analysand has learned in his bipersonal analysis, but he may also make further discoveries.

An analyst is sometimes asked by lay people whether they could analyse themselves if they had the necessary theoretical knowledge. They refer to Freud, who never had a bipersonal analysis. However, Freud did not only suffer from symptoms. He was also motivated by a thirst for knowledge, which can be found in pioneers, and he had a partner in self-analysis – his friend Fliess, with whom he discussed his findings orally and in writing. Freud also had conversations with other analysts and he could learn about himself from the work with his patients.

Every analyst who wants his interventions to reach a patient he works with must, to a certain extent, identify with the patient. For instance, he needs to do that in order to estimate the patient's limits of tolerance in regard to a certain intervention. With time, an analyst's capacity to empathically identify with another person will grow. Some things he sees in his patients he will already know from himself or from other people and he can be led to make new discoveries in himself and then understand phenomena in a patient that before had seemed inexplicable. Thus patient analysis will interact with an analyst's own analysis.

This book can be of use to people who have never been analysed and have never analysed anybody, but it is meant for former analysands. Of course, it may also help patients and candidates who are still in analysis to deal better with the self-analytic part of their analysis, which proceeds in the intervals between sessions. This book can also help a therapist to foster self-analytic capacities in his patients.

As in former books, I thank my patients, training analysands and supervisees for what I have learnt from them. I also owe much to my collaborators over the past fifteen years, who have worked with me in the department of group psychotherapy of Göttingen University, as well as many colleagues outside this department – whom I named in former books. I thank Erika Dzimalle and Elisabeth Wildhagen for fast and reliable typing, Susan Lathe for compiling the bibliography. Elisabeth Wildhagen, when critically reading the manuscript, acted as a model of common sense. I thank my wife Gisela and my son Peter for productive discussions.

CHAPTER ONE

The Working Relationship
in Self-Analysis

The concept of working alliance (Greenson 1967) refers to a situation where two people co-operate in therapy. Thus it may sound strange to use this concept for working with oneself. However, a person can indeed have a relationship with him or herself. You like yourself more or less, you permit yourself to do something or you are strict with yourself. A surgeon can do small surgery on himself. Some surgeons are even said to have removed their appendices with local anaesthesia. A doctor can take drugs to ease the symptoms of his flu or he can get himself into bed. On the other hand, you cannot pull yourself out of a swamp by pulling your hair.

Greenson's working alliance is probably the best-known concept of a therapeutic relationship alongside transference. I have applied the concept of working alliance or *working relationship* to a situation where more than two people are involved, as in group psychotherapy (König 1974; 1979).

The concept of working alliance has been an object of criticism (Brenner 1977; Körner 1989). Of course, working relationship and transference cannot be entirely separated. Both appear to be located on a continuum. The working alliance, as seen by Greenson, consists of the rational ego of the patient forming an alliance with the analysing ego of the analyst. Both are then trying to understand what happens in the patient's experiencing ego.

The concept of working alliance, as conceptualized by Greenson, already contains an element of self-analysis – perhaps this is even the concept's main rationale. On the level of the working alliance, the patient does not only accept the analyst's interventions or refuse to accept them. In an alliance with the analysing ego of the analyst, and identifying with the analyst as an analysing person, the analysand starts to do analysis by himself. For example, he may say that he is running away from something. Greenson used this as an example of a patient's utterances to show that a working relationship is beginning to be established.

In self-analysis after bipersonal analysis, the patient remains identified with the analyst's analysing ego. His self is in alliance with his inner imago of the analyst and the analysand continues the analytic process, observing himself and his behaviour in a way that is very similar to the way he did during analysis. Of course, his hypotheses will lack validation by the analyst. The self-analysand must validate his own hypotheses. While working through, the criteria for a good hypothesis will then consist of the changes achieved by putting it into practice.

Since the analysand must now address resistances without the analyst's help, his motivation for analysis becomes even more important than during bipersonal analysis. Symptoms may increase motivation. The self-analysand's being interested in himself as a person also contributes to motivation. This kind of motivation must be lacking in a self-analysand who feels that he is an uninteresting, unimportant person, as do many people with depressive character traits.

Something that will be lacking in self-analysis is the analyst's ability to see things more correctly than his analysand, because his blind spots do not, or only rarely, coincide with the analysand's. Also, a self-analysand cannot keep an hypothesis to him or herself, because he or she thinks the time has not yet come to inform the analysand about it. I shall take up this point in more detail later in this book.

Some resistances the self-analysand will never recognize, because they are so ego-syntonic. Among them there are resistances which an analyst in bipersonal analysis would recognize right away. For some reason, perhaps because the exterior living conditions were different, they may never have been addressed in bipersonal analysis. The self-analysand must largely leave the dosing of intervention to his own resistances. He may establish goals he wants to reach in self-analysis but he is often not able to see the ways to get there as well as an analyst who is less involved in the process. If you compare the analysing ego of the self-analysand and his experienced ego to two people playing chess, it becomes immediately apparent what problems exist. The self-analysand cannot split his ego (or his self) at will, producing a state of the self that might correspond to a multiple personality or to splitting in a borderline patient. As we all know, the borderline patient may be informed about what has happened before, without considering it to be relevant in the present situation, although it is relevant by what might be called normal criteria.

This kind of splitting is, of course, considered to be a pathological process. Sterba (1934), however, conceptualized a therapeutic split in the ego (the self), probably meaning that the ego of a patient can be in different consecutive states, but these ego states cannot keep information from one another.

In a bipersonal analysis the patient may remember something that has happened outside the hour, which he considered to be irrelevant at the time when it happened but that later may have become important. Of course, there are patients who always think or are even persecuted by the idea that everything they will do outside the analytic hour must be talked about during the hour, or at least that it could happen to be remembered. However, most people in analysis sometimes 'forget' that they are in analysis. Some deny it in order to be free to act as they please and they will perhaps 'forget' to mention things that happen between the hours. Similarly, a self-analysand may keep his memories separate from his analysing ego; a resistance that is easily recognized in bipersonal analysis but much more difficult to spot in self-analysis.

In a bipersonal analysis a patient's relationship with the analyst and his relations with objects outside analysis are addressed, as well as the analysand's relationship with himself. In self-analysis after termination, interactions with other people and the self-analysand's relationship with him or herself can be worked on as before, while the relationship with the analyst is now more or less a matter of the past. On the other hand, every analysand carries an internal imago of his analyst in his inner world, not only during analysis but also after termination. His relationship to this internal imago may change during the course of self-analysis. Thus the self-analysand may continue to work on his relationship with the analyst.

CHAPTER TWO

Ego-Syntonic Behaviour as a Problem

Behaviour is ego-syntonic when a person experiences his or her behaviour as normal for a person of his or her sex, age, profession and social position. Social stereotypes are often used in order to justify deficiencies ('I am a woman with no interest in technical matters, so I will not learn to change a wheel on my car' or 'A man's looks are not important, so I do not take care of my appearance.'). Character symptoms are often ego-syntonic, since the same behaviour, to a lesser degree, is socially acceptable. A scientist who takes no risks, is very careful in everything he or she does and always looks for somebody who could tell him or her what to do, may argue that reckless behaviour is dangerous, that caution is necessary in scientific work and that it is rational to look for people who are more experienced and can give advice as to the best course of action to be taken in a given situation.

Every person experiences conflicts between basic wishes, for example between the wish to realize one's potential on the job and the wish to spend time with one's family. Of course, wanting to realize one's potential on the job and wanting to be with one's family are normal wishes. A compromise may be found or one wish may be considered 'normal' and the other one pushed into the background. Thus a very ambitious person may say: 'Of course it's normal to want to realize one's potential' or a person who wants to be with his family to the point of neglecting his job may say: 'Of course it's normal to want to be with one's family'.

A person who stresses the 'normal' aspects of a certain kind of behaviour often does so in order to draw his and other people's attention away from other aspects of his behaviour. In self-analysis it is important to reflect on one's claims for normalcy.

CHAPTER THREE

Self-Analysis in Professional and Private Life

Psychotherapists engage in their work on a very personal level. General practitioners do the same, as well as people in the legal profession and in quite a few others.

The psychotherapist also uses himself as a person in order to arrive at a diagnosis. He examines what he feels and then tries to interpret it. General practitioners may learn in Balint groups how important it can be for the doctor–patient relationship to understand one's own reactions. They also learn that difficulties in relationships may be important signs that tell something about the patient, and about the doctor as well. This draws the attention of Balint group members to the *meaning* of their reactions.

An analytically-oriented psychotherapist uses his reactions all the time. In order to be able to do this he must know himself rather well. He learns about himself in personal analysis or in experiential groups. Difficulties in private life resulting from internal and interpersonal conflicts limit his capacity to use his reactions in a diagnostic way and to use the relationship with a patient in the service of therapy. When the therapist has terminated his personal analysis or experiential group he must rely on self-analysis in order to deal with such situations. Also, doing your job well or badly has an influence on your private life. Difficulties at work may reduce the capacity to relate to one's family. Many psychotherapists do self-analysis when problems in their work come up, but feel they have no time and energy left to reflect on private problems. Private problems, they feel, should be mastered without self-analysis!

Depressive therapists often turn to people who ask something from them and neglect people who do not ask for anything, and this may include themselves. Suppressed wishes, however, still exist and have an influence on the therapist's capacity to enjoy his work and to do it well. Many depressive therapists take on more patients if they have difficulties in their private lives in order to have a good reason for not tackling these problems. This may lead to the private problems increasing to a point where they cannot be ignored any longer because they now have a direct influence on the therapist's capacity to work with his patients. The therapist may then invest more energy in his work in order to remain successful, leaving even less energy for dealing with private problems. A vicious circle is established, which may result in separation from the family. At work, burn-out may result.

Of course, self-analysis is no panacea, but it can indeed interrupt the vicious circle that leads to private catastrophes and to professional burn-out.

CHAPTER FOUR

Transitional Situations

Like everybody else, therapists experience situations of transition that must be dealt with. A transitional situation is experienced in separation: from a partner, from children who leave home, taking leave from colleagues or from a boss.

Work of mourning may be necessary. An institution also acts as a global object which may be experienced as motherly. The boss is included in the global mother object or may have been experienced as a father object that protects the mother.

Places in one's relational network may be occupied or empty and, if they are occupied, the person in a certain place may fit more or less. In a new environment many places may remain empty for some time, or even forever. This is particularly true if a therapist leaves the hospital where he has worked in order now to practice psychotherapy in his own office. This type of work is, of course, much lonelier.

In such a transitional situation a therapist often makes demands on his partner to substitute what is missing and take on the roles of the missing persons, which he or she may not always want or be able to do.

In such a situation, or when a therapist's children leave home, he or she may be tempted to use patients as substitutes, expecting from them what he or she lost on an emotional level. This distorts a therapist's perception of his patients and is a frequent cause of countertransference problems (König 1993; 1995a; 1995b).

Transitional situations of another kind may also be very difficult, for example, 'taking leave' from physical competencies that diminish with advancing age but remain represented in a person's self-image. This situation can be very difficult to deal with and may have effect on a therapist's work, even if the competencies that now diminish have nothing to do with the competencies the therapist needs in his work – as is the case with being able to ski.

The transition from hospital work to a private practice diminishes the number of people one has contact with. Teaching at a psychoanalytic institute and taking part in its administration may compensate for this and partly explain the great importance an institute has for many of its members. Training analysands and supervisees may become very important for the training analyst and this may have repercussions on the way a training analysis or a supervision is conducted.

The training analyst's central position in a student's training may lead to the training analyst being regarded as the person who is responsible for him or her. training analysts may violate abstinence by giving analysands hints about how to behave in the seminars when they deal with a certain teacher. They may want to make the training analysands into their followers, who will later take their side in quarrels among the members of the institute. What can happen in training analysis can also happen in supervision, even more often, since less abstinence is considered to be necessary than in training analysis. On the other hand, aggressive transferences may be displaced from the training analyst to a supervisor, making life difficult for him, but idealizing transferences may also be displaced or appear by themselves, increasing the supervisor's influence on his student.

Self-analysis conducted by a training analyst or supervisor may contribute to prevent abuses of power, but there are difficulties. Abuse of power is often rationalized. A training analyst or supervisor seems to have good reasons for using power in just this way or he thinks violations of abstinence are in the service of training, just as sexual abuse by parents can be rationalized as sex education. Many traumatized people cannot imagine conducting their relationships in any other way, and this may also be the case for an analyst in a training analyst's or supervisor's role – especially when he has himself experienced abuse by his training analyst or supervisor and then takes his training analyst or supervisor as a model.

In private practice a therapist takes final responsibility for his therapies. Except in cases where he consults with a colleague, he must make many decisions by himself – more so than in a hospital, where he can talk with colleagues every day. Narcissistic therapists often experience little difference between hospital work and private practice, since they are used to expect much from themselves and little from others. Therapists with schizoid character traits often have difficulty in choosing the right treatment for a patient because they overlook important reality factors in a patient's life. Since they look through the psychic surface, as it were, they often have an intuitive understanding of a patient's psychodynamics. In a hospital, their neglect of reality factors is often compensated by colleagues or supervisors. In private practice these are now lacking and the therapist may soon be burdened with patients for whom the treatment he proposed is not appropriate. This may lead to outright failure in private practice. Some such therapists then try to return to a hospital position, or they restrict their indications in order to be on the safe side, which may work for them in a region where there is a small number of therapists and a large number of patients.

Therapists with strong depressive character traits are especially sensitive to a lack of personal relationships, and they may grow hungry for them. Depressive therapists feel stressed by ultimate responsibility. People and their welfare are important for them but their self-image as to professional competence is often devalued, which may affect their work.

Obsessive-compulsive therapists may conduct their practice in a ritualized and schematic way, thus trying to develop a feeling of safety, but to the detriment of therapeutic results.

Therapists with phobic character traits tend to take on self-confident patients who give them the illusion of being able to work for themselves, with the therapist accompanying them in their therapeutic endeavours.

Therapists with hysterical character traits may feel bad about having to conduct treatment from beginning to end, while in the hospital they were responsible for only part of the treatment. They also often lack the endurance a therapist in private practice should have if he or she does long-term therapy.

On the other hand, depressive therapists often feel better in private practice precisely because they need not separate from their patients after a short time. They may, however, keep the patients longer than necessary.

A therapist with depressive personality traits told me that it put a strain on him not to keep patients in hospital until they were cured. However, in private practice he had to take responsibility for termination. This put an even greater strain on him since he was now responsible for choosing the time when to separate from a patient, while in the hospital the responsibility of discharging patients before they were cured was made by his superiors.

Obsessive-compulsive analysts may feel responsible for a patient until he or she is 'completely' analysed, a state of affairs that, of course, never occurs. Obsessive-compulsive therapists with a need to control people feel responsible for the therapeutic process as it manifests itself outside the hour or even for the patient's whole life. On the one hand they feel good in private practice since they must not share responsibility with other people as in a hospital but, on the other hand, in a hospital, patients can be more completely controlled than in private practice.

CHAPTER FIVE

Self-Analysis in the Therapist's Couple Relationship

A therapist may experience difficulties in his or her private relationships, like other people do. Wishes that concern the therapist's parents are now directed to the partner. Father or mother or both are often expected to be substituted by his or her partner. Norms and values of different families may collide, especially if they are from different social strata.

Such conflicts may, however, hide oedipal pathology. A candidate who was a barber's son and had married a doctor's daughter was in analysis with a training analyst much interested in sociology. This training analyst referred the candidate's interpersonal conflicts with his wife to conflicts of norms and values derived from different social strata. He analysed the candidate's super-ego and ego ideal problems. After termination, the candidate, now an analyst, worked with a patient who was a shopkeeper's son. This patient was in the legal profession. He felt very uncomfortable with colleagues from an upper-middle-class background and felt he was not accepted by them as an equal. In working with his patient, the now analyst was able to see that his patient, coming from a background similar to his own, transferred a father object to his colleagues: the father not wanting his son to become his equal during the oedipal phase of his development. The analyst was now able to realize that the conflicts with his wife had an analogous basis. He transferred his mother, who had refused his oedipal advances.

A candidate's partner often experiences emotional and material deficits, hoping for change after her or his partner finishes training. Female candidates often postpone having children and, if they do have children, they must combine their training and their part in the children's upbringing with work in a hospital. Often there are conflicts with a spouse about the division of housework and of work that has to do with the children's upbringing.

After training there are no more seminars and there is less or no supervision. The analyst now treats more patients. He is more responsible for them since he cannot share his responsibility with a supervisor. In Germany, medical doctors who choose psychoanalysis as a profession accept that their income will be smaller than in other medical specialities. On the other hand, furnishing an office or waiting-room costs less than establishing a medical practice in another speciality. On the whole, one can say that most analysts and psychotherapists are satisfied with their choice of profession but they are not always able to transfer their satisfaction to their wives who may be more directly faced with economic difficulties. Some psychotherapists' or analysts' wives do not realize the drawbacks faced by the wives of doctors in other medical specialities (irregular hours, night calls, difficulties with the staff; a psychoanalyst just needs a receptionist and many work without one).

A psychoanalyst's wife whose first marriage was with a general practitioner told me that she enjoyed being able to sleep without being disturbed by night calls but she would have liked to change her car more often. She had also given up playing golf because of multiple conversations on the course about buying or using things she could not afford.

On the whole, psychoanalysts experience problems that are in some ways different from problems in other professions, but it is difficult to judge whether they have more, or more severe, problems. Maybe the problems are just different. One of the drawbacks in the pyschotherapeutic profession is that conflicts generated by a patient may become active in the therapist's couple relationship. Of course, it also happens in other professions that aggression caused at work is displaced onto the partner. However, as a rule, it is more difficult to find out whether a conflict arising in a psychotherapist's couple relationship has its causes in the couple relationship itself or in the therapist's relationship to one of his or her patients. Self-analysis should be started in time and may lead to the partners co-operating in solving the difficulty. Such co-operation between partners must, of course, be different from the fruitless talks about relationships shown in Woody Allen's films.

There is a danger of wrongly blaming a patient for 'causing' a specific conflict in a couple relationship. Reasons that stem from the couple relationship itself are then overlooked, which may lead to the conflict becoming chronic.

A conflict in a therapist couple may be caused by a person who relates to one of the partners, but this may have no effect on the couple relationship if the conflict was not preformed in the couple relationship. Often, latent conflicts become manifest by resonating with a conflict in the therapist's relationship with a patient. If therapists living together work in co-therapy, a conflict that was located in a couple may be activated *simultaneously* in both partners.

An analyst who did not get on well with his wife, who was an analyst herself, got into the habit of talking about his patients and the problems they caused him. His wife reciprocated. The couple spent an hour every evening talking about patients. Later on, the time spent on this increased to two hours on a working day and more on weekends. The couple also tried to analyse their interpersonal difficulties in terms of countertransference caused by their patients and displaced on the partner. They competed for the most plausible interpretations. When the wife told a friend about this, that lady was aghast at the amount of time the couple spent talking shop after a full day's work and said: 'But of course I have always known you as being very competitive and talking shop for such a long time will probably increase your competence, helping you to compete with your colleagues at the institute'. This started the couple talking about their competitiveness towards one another. It was often triggered by patients but it had been there all the time.

If a conflict is mobilized in one partner only, it will cause conflict in the couple relationship by modifying the behaviour of the therapist who perhaps now sees his partner in a different way. The partner may then be made an object of projective identification. The conflict may first arise in the inner world of the therapist, between one of the therapist's inner objects and parts of his self. One partner in the conflict may then be externalized and made real by projective identification. Of course, any conflicts in a therapist's couple relationship may have an influence on the work the therapist does with patients (König 1995b).

Oedipal conflicts mobilized by a patient in one of the partners may concern his or her parents and parents-in-law. A husband may start to feel jealous of his wife's father; the wife may start to feel jealous of her husband's mother.

Conflicts can primarily concern people outside the therapist's family. For example, the husband may have a fantasy of being treated in an unfriendly way by the porter in a hotel. Amplifying his fantasy, he makes himself into a rich man who buys the hotel and fires the porter. Also, the hotel may represent the wife and the porter represent her father.

Another husband may have a fantasy of being stronger than it appears. This is a frequent fantasy of oedipal children. In adults there may be fantasies of having a small, cheap looking car which has a very strong motor that makes it run faster than much bigger and more expensive cars. On the whole, daydreams seem to occur frequently in couple conflicts and can yield much diagnostic material.

The fact that daydreams play an important role in couple conflicts may have something to do with a wish to hold the conflict with a person who plays an important part in one's life at bay as long as possible but permit it to come up in fantasy. In self-analysis a conflict may be recognized in a partner's daydream before it has had a detrimental effect on the couple relationship.

A therapist, working in an outpatient department, started to day-dream about having sex with a receptionist on the same floor. He never talked to her in private. They just met on the corridor and exchanged greetings. The therapist had had a very over-protective, intruding mother and had married a girl who was very fond of him, wanted to spend much time with him, asked him how he felt when he came home from work and could she perhaps do something for him to make him happy? The therapist loved his wife and liked to spend time with her. He considered his wife's questioning of him to be a sign of her affection – indeed, he was disappointed when his wife did not ask him how he had spent the day and how he was feeling.

However, the frequency of intercourse in his marriage was diminishing. He blamed this on the amount of work he had to do. One day, after he had finished his work, he stayed at his desk for a while and fantasized about having sex with the receptionist in his colleague's office. The discrepancy between his sexual fantasies and the lack of attraction he felt for his wife became apparent to him. He did not feel too tired to indulge in sexual fantasies, but too tired to sleep with his wife. His wife did things for him and cared for him so much, while the receptionist showed hardly any interest in him at all. It then dawned on the therapist that it was perhaps the distance between the receptionist and himself, and her lack of interest in him, that made her attractive. He was able to make a connection between his attitude towards his wife and his attitude towards his mother, who pestered him with questions when he came home from school.

A reason for fantasies being prominent in a couple relationship may be that the partners have withdrawn from one another and now fantasize about things they would otherwise have brought up in conversation.

In self-analysis one may concede more than in couple therapy. Being 'right' is not as important as when actually fighting with one's partner. Of course, interpersonal conflicts in couple relationships may have very bad consequences. Thus partners often do much in order to avoid them – especially if their professional work absorbs much energy and time, as with a therapist who wants to do good work with his patients and keep up with the professional literature. Outright denial and playing down of conflicts are often employed and sometimes displacement on patients occurs. Projective identification of the communicative type (König 1995b) is employed in order to create states of feeling in the other person 'similar to one's own' that would not occur spontaneously. Often the partners just withdraw from one another.

Emotional withdrawal in a couple relationship is often difficult to bear. It may cause a therapist to direct his emotional needs towards his patients. A colleague told me that he seemed to be able better to tolerate his workload when his wife withdrew emotionally after a fight, continuing to do so for several weeks, because he liked his patients more when his wife was sulking. Many therapist couples fight regularly about one and the same issue. Aggression is vented, but to no consequence. The partners have learned to deal with a fight about this particular issue. Such fights may take the heat off a conflict but they do nothing to solve it.

In couple relationships of therapists, problems of social status are often important. I have rarely found therapist couples where both partners work about the same amount of time and share housework and the children's upbringing in equal parts. Such an arrangement functions best if paid helpers or helpful relatives are available. Some couples share the children's upbringing with other couples. Paid helpers are usually less problematic.

If the partners do different amounts of professional work, the one who works less may gain less professional status, or even lose some. His attention is then directed to status problems. The partner with a lower professional status may try to devalue what his or her partner, who does more professional work, has achieved, in order to reach a balance. This aspect of couple relationships is treated in more detail in König and Kreische (1991), along with other topics that concern problems in couple relationships.

CHAPTER SIX

Self-Analysis and One's Children

Psychotherapists often think they are experts in developmental psychology and therefore experts in dealing with children. They may feel worse than other people when their children do not thrive as they feel they should. This may be one of the reasons why some psychotherapists find it difficult to have children at all. They are afraid of a task they consider to be difficult, of failure and of the narcissistic injury it would entail. Often there are conflicts between norms and values that are derived from the wife's and the husband's primary family or from the wife's and the husband's peer groups. This is, for example, true for the goals one should have in life, whether one should want to care for people or develop one's gifts. In dealing with children the personality structures of parents are also important. For instance, depressive people long to be in the presence of important objects, and children are such objects.

Narcissistic parents often prefer to be on their own. Obsessive-compulsive and phobic parents fear the children's potential of causing havoc or they fear that an accident might happen to them. Hysterical parents activate oedipal conflicts by acting seductively. Schizoids may rather perceive 'the child as such' than a particular child with his or her individual character traits.

The idea that parents must 'offer' a good life to their children – probably more prevalent in therapists couples than in others – may lead to the parents overtaxing themselves emotionally and sometimes also economically. Parents may put their own wishes and desires so far into the background that this causes aggression in them, which must be hidden from the children. If suppressed aggression comes out in aggressive acts, most parents will try to compensate by doing even more for their children, thereby increasing their own latent aggression. Some parents try to escape the burden their children seem to impose on them by trying to find a different partner or just sleeping with another person. Home is a place where one is overtaxed. Home becomes unattractive and adverse emotional reactions are generalized to include the partner one lives with.

Self-analysis should concentrate on ideologies stemming from the primary families, on aspects of one's personality structure that may generate conflicts and on norms, values and relational models from one's own primary family. Some parents behave the way they do because they want to be better parents than their father and mother. They then often behave in a way contrary to their parent's behaviour. Here, oedipal conflicts may come in.

In quite a few couples, the main issue in dealing with children is control. In such couples the wish to control a situation is usually ubiquitous, not confined to dealing with children. The differences between the ways both parents want to deal with their children may be minimal. Control must be achieved. Obsessive-compulsive people feel powerless if they do not win control. Also, self-esteem may depend on winning. In sports often a few hundredths of a second decide victory or defeat. In my experience conflicts that depend on major differences in the positions a man or a woman take in a couple relationship can be more easily dealt with and compromises can more easily be found than if the conflict is about small matters. Major differences can be explained by different interests or different biographies. They can often be rationally worked out and finally resolved. If there are small differences, the quarrel is about who wins. Working on the motives for such behaviour is a difficult task.

CHAPTER SEVEN

Technical Hints

Freud (1900) was the first person to analyse himself. Of course, he had someone, Fliess, with whom he talked and to whom he wrote about self-analysis – perhaps Fliess was present in Freud's imagination when he did self-analysis. A self-analysand in our times may succeed in a similar way. Perhaps it was important that Fliess and Freud did not live in the same city, which probably made it easier to be open about the results of a self-analysis than if Fliess had lived in Vienna.

The 'royal road' of dream analysis can only be used in self-analysis if certain preconditions are observed. It is important to see Freud as a scientist doing original research on himself. This kind of motivation is lacking in most of today's psychotherapists. The researcher should try to be as objective as possible. Of course, this holds true even today but we have become less optimistic about our capacity to think and react objectively. Freud's idea of a research psychologist is contained in the metaphor of the mirror, the therapist reflecting the patient's behaviour back to him without distorting it by his own subjectivity. Today we know that this is not possible to the degree Freud thought was attainable (see Habermas 1975). In analysing one's own dreams, subjective factors play an even bigger role.

Since the 'royal road' of dream analysis is fraught with considerable difficulties, other roads should also be explored. Calder (1980) proposed to analyse micro symptoms, looking at the situation in which they occur. Micro symptoms are parapraxes, affects and moods that do not seem to fit the present situation. Luborsky (1984) added psycho-somatic symptoms like headaches or stomach aches.

Some parapraxes are due to suppression, that is, to pushing feelings or impulses to act out of one's mind, not to repression, which is an unconsciously triggered mechanism of defence. The analysis of parapraxis due to suppression is comparatively easy but does not lead to new insights. However, suppression and repression can link together. I once said 'goodbye' on receiving a particularly difficult patient with bad eyesight. On analysing my parapraxis, I identified it as a counter-transference reaction but did not gain access to any hitherto uncon-scious reason for wishing the patient off. He was difficult because he was very resistive. Otherwise, I even liked him. However, on thinking further about the patient, I considered his bad eyesight. My mother had suffered from bad eyesight in the later years of her life. She had also become somewhat difficult. My transference to the patient came on top of his being resistive.

Exploration of a situation in which a micro symptom occurs usually starts with establishing proximity in time. If micro symptoms appear several times in the same kind of situation or closely before or after it, a causal nexus may be supposed to exist. In logical reasoning, the deduction '*post hoc, ergo propter hoc*' (one occurrence follows another in time, therefore it follows from it) is not admitted.

This, however, only holds true for deductive reasoning. In inductive reasoning two events closely linked in time are usually considered to be in some way causally connected. This is often affirmed by statistics, but a statistical computation that does not lead to significant results cannot be used as a proof against the existence of a causal connection. '*Post hoc, ergo propter hoc*' is often true in closed or semi-closed systems.

If unpleasant events occur along with certain situations, it seems sensible to avoid such situations. In fact, most people act accordingly. If they get a stomach ache or diarrhoea after ingesting certain foods, they will probably avoid them in the future – and this in cases where the food itself has nothing to do with the illness as it was caused by bacteria that multiplied because the food was kept too long in the fridge. The right thing to do would be not to avoid the food but to avoid keeping it too long before eating it. Of course, it takes more knowledge and more reasoning to arrive at such a conclusion.

We deal with psychological symptoms in similar ways. Agoraphobics avoid the street. They can observe that anxiety diminishes when somebody accompanies them and may then look for somebody willing and able to do so. Of course, agoraphobics at this stage will not know the mechanisms of this. They will just feel safer and experience less anxiety if accompanied. In an analysis an agoraphobic may find out that his companion or 'directing object' (König 1981) protects him from succumbing to sexual or aggressive temptation which he might face walking in the street. We know that explaining this to a patient is usually of no effect. The patient must discover this information in himself. If the information is just given by the therapist, he will in most cases either refuse it or agree with it without being convinced. Here, as in many other situations, there is a great difference between having something described by another person and experiencing it oneself.

In self-analysis knowledge by direct experience must be obtained in order to effect changes. Knowledge by description is in everyday language often labelled 'theoretical'. Such 'theoretical knowledge' in many cases exerts no influence on the way we act.

Self-analysis does not usually reach so far as to entirely clarify the connections between a situation that triggers a symptom, linking both to the person's psychodynamics. Theoretical knowledge can then be used tentatively to establish links between the phenomena observed. In this case, theoretical knowledge establishes a connection between two phenomena, somewhat similar to a metal plate used to reconnect the fragments of a broken bone; such a metal plate does not establish total stability, but conditions for establishing a firm connection are improved. In a bipersonal analysis tentative links are established by the therapist's interventions. For example, a therapist may offer an interpretation that establishes a link between two phenomena a patient experiences as separate. Stability can then usually be reached by working through.

In self-analysis, theoretical knowledge that seems to fit, having a certain face validity, may be used in situations that trigger symptoms in order to explore what happened. Establishing psychodynamic links will cause such situations to be looked at in a different way and this will then result in different reactions to an analogous situation that occurs later on. A colleague once told me that on reading an article of mine on fixation in adolescence causing grown-up people still to act like adolescents in certain ways, he considered his way of dressing and suddenly realized that, compared to other people in his profession, he dressed much younger – in fact, in some ways like an adolescent. He also realized that a tendency to rebel against authority, which he had ascribed to oedipal problems not resolved during his own analysis, was really more similar to an adolescent's behaviour, identifying with people outside the family and thinking that his parents were too old-fashioned and unnecessarily strict.

When psychodynamic links have become clear, it is easier to be aware of a lack of competencies that would be needed in order maturely to deal with a situation which causes anxiety. For example, a woman can discover that a lack of practice in dealing with men makes it difficult for her to refuse a man's proposal to have sex without damaging a professional relationship. A woman who becomes aware of such a lack of social routine could imagine situations that make it necessary to refuse a man and think about the ways she might choose to proceed. She can also examine solutions represented in novels, in films or on television. She might look for situations to practise dealing with men, for example by joining a club or an association of some kind that concentrates on some activity like sports, but also offers opportunities for social intercourse.

In self-analysis that addresses character it is especially important to be aware of one's concept of normality and to reflect on it. In my view (König 1992; König and Lindner 1994), ideal human behaviour cannot exist. What is best in a certain situation depends on the situation itself, the social environment – especially the social stratum a person lives in – and perhaps the social position he or she wants to reach. It depends on professional role and the kind of people you work with. Different professions demand different competencies and presuppose different interests that make for different norms and values. A society where work is differentiated can hardly be imagined without different inclinations of persons who do different kinds of work. Inclinations to do certain types of work depend, among other things, on personality structure.

Many people are highly motivated to think of their own behaviour as normal. They feel there is no need to change 'normal' behaviour, even if it has some disadvantages. However, even in these people, some disadvantageous ways of experiencing relationships or of acting in relationships, as well as difficulties in doing everyday work, may provide a motivation to ameliorate things. It is normal that a person who is out of training cannot do sports as well as someone who is well trained. Similarly, a therapist's problems in working with difficult patients may be called normal but he or she may nevertheless want to do the work better and with less exertion.

Some people do not want to change because they fear failure. They are afraid that their attempts at changing might fail. This may concern change of any kind. Of course, 'normal' behaviour could be changed more easily if another kind of 'normal' behaviour were immediately available as a substitute.

A colleague told me that, trying to learn Russian in order to be able to read the great Russian novelists, he found it difficult to adapt to the Cyrillic letters. He thought he had no alternative. The phonetic signs used to transcribe Cyrillic print were just as bad. Then he hit on a book that transcribed Cyrillic writing using the letters he was accustomed to from his own language. With the book went a tape recording. He had bought this book at a railway station, not knowing what the system was. When on the train, he found this out and thought it was silly. Using the German letters seemed a superfluous detour to him, and of course they could not really render the Russian pronunciation. However, he started reading the transcribed dialogues and listening to the tape and within a short time he found out that this method was for him. His own reluctance to learn Russian because of the difficulty caused by the Cyrillic letters was now easy to overcome. He learned to pronounce the words he had listened to from the transcription and, on looking at a word in Cyrillic writing, he recognized it at once. Later on he found out that his aversion to Cyrillic letters had been caused by the signs the Russian occupational army had put up in the town where he lived as a small boy at the end of World War II.

Similarly, a detour can often be helpful in analysing a certain problem. Also, it is sometimes easier to recognize a problem after having heard or read it described in a lecture, article or book. Several colleagues have told me that their self-analysis was helped by reading case histories as well as by working with patients.

Being normal may be experienced as a disadvantage. This holds true for competencies and talents. It may hurt to realize that one's talent for music or writing is normal, in the sense of being average. Some people with high talents feel that they should be able to achieve everything without work. For them, realizing that they are normal in the sense that they must work may entail narcissistic injury. On the other hand, therapy and also self-analysis can make people with low self-esteem realize their talents; it can also help to see one's limits and come to terms with them.

Most people are helped in exploring their personality structure by realizing that every personality structure has advantages and drawbacks and what they are. Colleagues told me that they found descriptions of personality structures helpful. Of course, much was familiar to them, but some information they had ignored, either because they were not in a position to bear confrontation with certain aspects of their personality or because it did not concern the patients they treated at that time and they could not realize that it concerned themselves. Of course, every therapist, while doing therapy, encounters information that concerns him personally. So-called blind spots may keep him from realizing this.

I shall now give an example by describing two kinds of wishes that go in the same direction and yet are fundamentally different. There is a difference between the wish to have control and the wish to exert influence. Somebody who wants control will want to make all decisions himself. Somebody who wants to exert influence will just want to have influence on other people's decisions. He does not wish to have total control but wants his own needs and wishes to be taken into consideration. Most people want to have influence. They want to have their needs and wishes taken up and considered without expecting that they get *everything* they wish for. Somebody who wants control wants to be in a position that makes it possible for him to decide in the last resort what will be done. This must not necessarily mean that only his ideas and no others should be used. Ideas from other people can be used and integrated but the powerful person who is in control wants to decide finally what will happen, even if he or she uses other people's ideas.

A person who wants total control is in constant danger of losing it, while a person who wants influence may see his influence diminish without feeling totally powerless. Just one single person who refuses to be controlled and succeeds in putting his or her own ideas into practice will topple a person who wants total control. Someone who wants total control must experience every independent action as directed against him or herself. He or she must fear other people's acts of independence much more than somebody who just wants to have influence.

Everyone with experiences in bipersonal analysis can remember instances where he realized that experiences from the past had made him misunderstand a certain situation and draw wrong conclusions. He will remember having reacted to a present person as he reacted to a person in the past. There may have been some real similarities but these were exaggerated to make the present person fit the past one. Working on the assumption that this might be so, the analysand arrived at a more realistic view of the other person.

Of course, it is easy to find and name instances where such misjudgements may have dire consequences, for example in choosing a partner or in dealing with a partner. Transference can lead a person to leave his or her job because of conflicts with the boss that have their roots in his or her own past.

Someone may want to obtain a certain job because he transfers a mother object on an institution or because he transfers a good father object to its manager. People may stay on in a job they should leave on rational considerations, but do not give up because the business they work in has taken on motherly or fatherly functions he or she fears not to be able to find in any other job.

In bipersonal analysis regression will foster transferences of infantile objects, not only during the sessions but also between the sessions. As explained elsewhere (König and Lindner 1994), regression between the sessions is less in group psychotherapy than in individual analysis. Aspects of infantile objects also co-determine our non-regressed everyday behaviour.

Sometimes we experience inadequate or overly intense emotions that can make one think of infantile influences without being experienced as outright ego-dystonic. In a bipersonal analysis it is the analyst who can then confront the analysand with the incongruousness of these feelings and name possible reasons for them. In self-analysis there is no other person who can do this. If not addressed, incongruous or over-intensive feelings may be rationalized, suppressed, repressed or, with time, recede into the background and finally be forgotten.

Of course, if feelings are very strong, but still not ego-dystonic, an analysand may react angrily to his analyst's confrontations. A good working relationship can sometimes be covered up by transference. Even when transference is to external objects, ego-functions can be paralyzed by intense feelings.

In self-analysis it is a good rule to reflect on all intense feelings that occur. Some intense feelings may have realistic reasons but one has to analyse them in order to learn whether they are realistic or not. I once got quite angry at a student who had difficulties in finishing her doctoral dissertation, which was part of a larger project planned for joint publication. At first I thought that my anger was fully justified by publication being delayed. Then I realized that I was angry at the reasons she gave for her difficulties, which were similar to the reasons an important person in my past had given.

Reflecting on all intense feelings can have its drawbacks – for example in a romantic relationship, where too much reflection may stifle spontaneous feelings. On the other hand, reflecting on one's feelings can prevent wrong decisions that may turn out to have dire consequences not only for oneself but also for the partner, as can happen in intercourse without a condom. We all move on a continuum between not wanting to engage ourselves emotionally and letting emotions take over.

Transference may confine itself to certain aspects of a person in one's past, and every transference can work from the unconscious. We all know that it is one of the most important aspects of transference that one is not aware of it. In self-analysis it is often very difficult to make the connection with aspects of the past that have become unconscious, as an analyst in bipersonal analysis does using reconstruction.

It is important to realize that ideal objects can be transferred, ideal objects that are in some ways the contrary of what was experienced. For example, an ideal mother may be a warm, generous and giving person, while the real mother was cool and refused to give much.

Of course, not all transferences cause intense feelings that have an adverse effect on thinking. Some transferences just make us misjudge another person. For example, somebody may idealize his boss who he or she thinks will act like his father by refusing to lay him or her off in an economic crisis. Such a person may be totally surprised if fired. Of course, the boss would not have fired his son or daughter, or he would have provided for him or her in other ways, but he will usually fire his employee in a crisis, even if this is emotionally difficult for him. In such cases transference may prevent a person from looking for a more stable job or from making provisions for a period of unemployment.

Intense feelings as a result of transference may occur *when transference expectations turn out to be erroneous*. Of course, similar behaviour may have its roots in personality structure. Some people have a naïve trust in other people, this holds true for persons with schizoid or hysterical character traits. Trusting a boss who one feels will act like an ideal father is no less unrealistic than fighting with a boss one feels is similar to an authoritarian father experienced during childhood.

Acting in unrealistic ways that are determined by personality structure is often buttressed by ideology and thus kept ego-syntonic: 'All people should act this way.' Even if a person considers his own behaviour as just one of several ways of behaving that can all lay a claim to normality, he or she may still feel that they are a bit more normal and a bit more right than people who behave in other normal ways. Ideologies can be used to attempt to justify asocial behaviour, like robbing a bank in order to obtain funds for political work or, to take a more frequently occurring instance, spurious arguments may be used to obtain a job for a person who shares one's political convictions.

Many people who refer to ideology in order to justify their behaviour do so abusively. In psychoanalytic institutes there may be fights in the name of psychoanalysis, where psychoanalysis is a science that must be promoted and kept 'pure' is misused to cover personal needs and interests, for example the need to be in control. Since there is no therapeutic contract among colleagues, personal motives should not be interpreted. Colleagues must often be content to fight on the ideological level proposed by the adversary.

People who buttress their arguments with ideology often find it very difficult to question them in self-analysis. If they did so, they would feel a traitor to the ideological positions they support and fight for.

There is a technical procedure that can help to recognize transference. It consists of comparing the person in one's present relational network to the persons in one's primary family. Doing this systematically helps to discover transferences of the conscious aspects of internal objects in relationships where one just did not want to take this into consideration. In self-analysis there are certain advantages in substituting the boundaries and rules of the setting as introduced, established and defended by the analyst by one's own set of systematic procedures.

The way one deals with these procedures, following them or 'forgetting' them or refusing to follow them 'just in this instance', can be analysed. Resistances will point to important contents one would have overlooked without having established certain rules and having resolved to follow them.

CHAPTER EIGHT

Free Association in Self-Analysis

Most colleagues with whom I have talked about self-analysis do not lay down on a couch in order to free associate, like they did in their bipersonal analysis. Most of those who do start their self-analytic work from some determined point: a patient, a relative, a dream, something that happened, an emotion (affect, mood or body feeling). Calder (1980) seems to work in a similar way, finding associations to dreams less useful than he had expected. As mentioned before in this book, he found it useful to depart from micro symptoms; that is, symptoms of small intensity and limited duration.

Such symptoms occur in specific situations and, as a rule, disappear spontaneously. Associations can be to symptoms, but also to the situation where the symptom occurred. More serious symptoms – in the case of Junker (1993), who described his reanalysis, it was bronchial asthma – can usually not be dealt with in self-analysis, except as a preparation for bipersonal treatment. Of course, self-analysis of physical symptoms should not preclude physical examination. Self-analysis may act as a resistance against medical exploration, the results of which one is afraid of. Self-analysis can also be a resistance against starting bipersonal treatment.

The limits of self-analysis often show up in the difficulties encountered in dealing with stops or detours in free association that have something to do with the contents one is approaching. In bipersonal analysis the analyst can substitute for the ego functions that are paralyzed by the conflict that is approached. In self-analysis it may be better to change over to another aspect of a situation where micro symptoms occurred, thus circling around the problem and approaching it gradually from several directions.

In self-analysis, as in bipersonal analysis, associations can lead astray. For example, a person on whom aggressive feelings are displaced that were originally directed towards another living person may be connected to people long dead or to people one has separated from. The associations do not concern the important person in the present, from whom the aggressive feelings have been displaced. It may be true that they were originally displaced from a person in the past but they now concern a person in the present. The person from the past one remembers has something to do with the whole situation, but it is an error of omission to think only of that person. Manifest aggression against the present person can, however, be diminished when a connection between the original source of displacement and the person the aggression is consecutively displaced on is established. This may lead to improvements that remain, however, suboptimal. In bipersonal analysis the analyst would perhaps have noticed that an important present person was circumvented in the analysand's associations.

Summing up, one can say that in self-analysis, as in bipersonal analysis, stereotyped and exclusive thinking about persons from the past may be in the service of avoiding displeasure induced by dealing with a present person.

Sometimes associations to a patient lead to the therapist himself. Identifications with a patient can thus be discovered. These identifications can stem from various stages of the therapist's development: from the present as well as from childhood or adolescence. There are, of course, instances when associations about a patient lead to oneself because one takes a father's or mother's position which, if it is done without reflecting on it, may endanger therapy by removing the therapist from his professional, impartial role. One cannot *successfully* do psychotherapy with one's own children and it is difficult to treat a patient if one keeps feeling like a real father or mother to him (König 1993; 1995b).

CHAPTER NINE

Feedback

Feedback consists in telling other people about one's reactions to them. Feedback can be verbal or non-verbal. It can be intended or just happen. This section is about intended feedback. People on the receiving end of feedback often defend against it by rationalization. They say: 'This he (or she) just says because …'. In a strict sense, rationalizing means explaining one's own behaviour as rational, neglecting irrational motives. If somebody says that another person rationalizes, he or she usually means that the other person gives false rational reasons for his or her behaviour because he or she has strong emotional reasons not to be objective, for example only seeing what is bad and ignoring what is good. This holds true for negative feedback but, of course, positive feedback can also be refused. Depressive people with low self-esteem will not accept positive feedback if it is too far removed from their self concept, they may then also say 'He says this only because …'. For example, they may think: 'He only says this because he needs me, because he wants something from me or because he tries to appear friendly'. A refusal of negative feedback may be explained by the person giving that feedback being envious, competitive or for some other reason unable to notice or admit good things in other people – only seeing the bad ones.

A depressive person may defend against positive feedback in order to avoid cognitive dissonances that occur because self concept and feedback are too different from one another, while negative feedback is seen as a validation of the depressive person's self concept. However, if negative feedback is much more negative than his or her self concept, the depressive person may refuse it. Thus very negative feedback can cause a depressive person to argue against it and change his or her self concept, for example thinking and perhaps saying: 'I'm not *that* stupid'.

Persons with depressive character traits may fear positive feedback because they experience it as implicitly containing demands for the future. Having passed an exam with good grades, they feel that they must pass all future exams with grades that are as good or better. In this they feel they will not be able to succeed. Positive feedback may increase such a person's negative attitudes towards him or herself. He or she may then think: 'I shouldn't have passed this exam, at least not with these grades, in reality I know almost nothing. The person who examined me must have made a mistake or he (or she) just likes me. In any case, I cannot be as good as he (or she) makes me appear to be'.

Narcissistic people take positive feedback as a validation of their self concept. Often they feel that it is not positive enough. They may then think: 'This fellow does not want to say what he *really* thinks of me because ...'. However, a very positive feedback can drive a narcissistically structured person into a state of narcissistic excitation, which he or she experiences as unpleasant because it is accompanied by fantasies of omnipotence that are experienced as dangerous.

Narcissistic people often do not let negative feedback touch them. If, however, their self concept is not stable or has recently been doubted, negative feedback may lead to narcissistic injury. Of course, everybody can be injured by negative feedback. However, a narcissistic person's reaction is often very intense, usually more intense than the person who gave the negative feedback expected. In some relationships, for example in some fighting couples, negative feedback is intended to hurt very much. The predisposition to narcissistic injury is here taken into account.

Feedback occurs in therapies, especially in group therapy, and also in daily life where there usually is no *therapeutic* intention, although feedback is often given in order to effect change by an act of will on the receiver's side. In daily life, negative feedback is more frequent than positive. Positive feedback is most often given by people who are in love with the other person. Such feedback may seem exaggerated to an impartial observer. On the other hand, hatred can motivate feedback that is easily recognized as being exaggerated and intended to hurt. Giving feedback is often experienced as difficult. Positive feedback is more easily given by a person who feels he or she is in a superior position – for example as a guest in a restaurant (most positive feedback in restaurants seems to be about the quality of food, being in principle directed to the cook who is not present and only indirectly to the waitress or to the waiter insofar as they work in a place where good food is cooked, which may increase their self-esteem).

Feedback is often used for manipulative purposes, less so in therapeutic groups where manipulation can be more freely addressed than in daily life. For example, people give positive feedback in a restaurant in order to be well served next time. Another motive to give positive feedback is a wish to identify with the receiver of feedback in his pleasure at receiving it. This motive often occurs in people who have a tendency to use altruistic delegation (Sandler and Freud 1985). Such persons have difficulty in experiencing pleasure or joy, they can do it more easily by *identifying* with people who are experiencing it.

Positive feedback may be intended to make a relationship better or to stress one's superior position, judging the other person. Feedback in daily life is, as a rule, less objective than in group psychotherapy where participants and, of course, the therapist feel obliged to try to be objective in the service of therapy.

As in groups, in daily life outside therapy people who want to be *useful* to another person by giving feedback may make a conscious effort to be objective.

In experiential groups positive feedback is rarely questioned. This may relate to an implicit agreement to help one another, which includes encouragement and support. However, not questioning positive feedback often works against therapy. Thus group members may behave towards a middle-aged woman as if she were much younger, thereby buttressing her illusion that she has much time left to look for a partner. Of course, every feedback can be distorted by idealization, devaluation, love or hate. In a therapy group, just as in daily life, people can rally against a group member or subgroup thus addressing what is problematic in themselves. Feedback may be based on projection, but also on introjection. If an object you deal with is introjected, everything you say about the object also addresses yourself.

Feedback of any kind can be intended to have specific effects, to produce a change of behaviour or just an emotional reaction like joy or narcissistic hurt. Negative feedback can be used to change power relations by diminishing or 'destroying' the adversary. Both negative and positive feedback can be an expression of one's affects or moods. A person can try to get something off his chest by saying what makes him angry in another person. People 'running over from joy' may want to express this feeling by saying that they love just everybody in the room, implying that everybody is loveable.

On the whole, one is well advised to view feedback with a critical eye, taking the motivation of the feedback giver into account. On the other hand, a hypercritical attitude has its drawbacks, reducing pleasure caused by positive feedback and preventing the use of a negative feedback for improving one's behaviour by reflecting on the reasons for it.

As mentioned above, a refusal feedback can be explained by assuming rationalization. On the other hand, rationalization is not only used in order to diminish a feedback's effects, presupposing manipulative motives in the person who gave the feedback. One's own rational motives to accept feedback or to refuse it will not always tell the whole story. Thus one may say: 'I refuse this positive feedback because I'm realistically critical of myself' or 'I know myself best, therefore other people's negative opinions about myself are not relevant'.

Feedback can most easily be accepted if it contains observations and personal reactions but not interpretations. If a wife says: 'I'm not your mother', this may be considered an interpretation. A link is established between the husband's behaviour in relationship to a mother and the husband's behaviour in relationship to his wife. The feedback, 'You make me do this as if you could not do it yourself' is a description; 'You behave as if you could not do this yourself in order to make me do it and avoid the work' is an interpretation. If somebody says, 'I'm angry because …' he describes an affect and gives reasons for it, perhaps referring to another person's behaviour.

Somebody who interprets conveys, among other things, that he knows better than the other person. A feedback without an interpretation usually contains an injunction to change. It is usually not said how a person could achieve change. The feedback 'I'm not your mother' can be seen as containing the injunction 'please realize that you behave towards me as if I were your mother. Behave towards me as the person I am'.

If the wife who says, 'I'm not your mother' lives with her husband and his mother in the same house or if the mother, when on a visit, does certain things for the husband, the feedback may not contain much interpretation. Saying, 'I'm not your mother' may just mean that the mother does certain things for the husband which his wife does not want to do for him.

However, if the husband's mother is absent or dead, the feedback may contain more interpretation. It may be meant to convey that the wife experiences her husband like a child and herself like a grown-up person. If the woman has some knowledge of psychoanalysis, the feedback, 'I'm not your mother' may in fact mean that she considers her husband not to be able to live in a mature relationship, being arrested in his development and showing infantile behaviour which he should realize, understand and change. In this case, the husband will probably react in an adverse way – especially if he understands what his wife meant to convey. He may then say: 'You should not always interpret', instead of perhaps using the wife's feedback in his self-analysis.

CHAPTER TEN

Self-Analysis and Projective Identification

A person who transfers an object or externalizes a part of his self on another person may unconsciously manipulate that other person in a way to make him or her conform to his expectations. Transference or externalization are thus validated in reality. There are various motives for this, for example there may be a wish to re-encounter familiar behaviour in another person. The behaviour is familiar because it is similar to the behaviour of a person from whom an internal object is derived or similar to the way one behaves or would, consciously or unconsciously, like to behave. I call this projective identification of the transference type.

A person may want to transform a conflict into an interpersonal one in order to ease conflicts in his inner world. I call this projective identification of the conflict relieving type.

The motive may be to make the other person experience one's own feelings in order to facilitate communication. I call this projective identification of the communicative type. On the other hand, a person may fear to be well understood because this might mobilize fear of re-fusion. He or she may then projectively identify the other person with an object that lacks empathy or he or she experiences as very different from him or herself. I call this the separation type of projective identification.

It is important to be clear about the meaning of the word 'identification' as used in this context. Here, identification does not mean that a person's identity is established ('he was identified as the burglar') nor does it mean empathic understanding ('I identify with a patient') or adapting one's behaviour to the behaviour of another person (identifying with the protagonist in a cowboy film, you walk like him when leaving the cinema). Here, identifying means that another person's behaviour is adapted to a concept one has of him or her.

A therapist can be projectively identified but he can also projectively identify a patient. The former is easier to recognize, especially if the patient's inner object or the part of the patient's self one is identified with, stems from early stages of life and therefore has archaic qualities. It is extremely difficult to recognize one's own projective identifications since projective identification is a defence mechanism which is triggered unconsciously and is *meant* to distort perception. In a bipersonal analysis the analyst can help. In self-analysis, one way of recognizing one's own projective identifications is to use feedbacks from people one projectively identifies or from people who observe this. The feedbacks must concern the interpersonal part of projective identification. Therapists who have participated in self experience groups are at an advantage because they have been trained in using feedbacks. A 'suitable' choice of people one deals with can cause the same effects as projective identification: people need not be manipulated into doing things they do by themselves, they were chosen for this. Such partner choices can be recognized easily if they repeat themselves.

At the beginning of a relationship, projective identification is often not necessary if people give very little information about themselves. It becomes necessary when the amount of information increases, highlighting differences from what was expected. Again, this does not hold true for borderline patients with very archaic inner objects and self representations since reticent behaviour is often not what such patients expect, they expect very clear-cut behaviour traits.

Some people can be projectively identified quite easily, as can persons with a histrionic streak. They tend to take on roles that are offered to them, reacting to minimal signals. However, they usually do not stay in one role for long. This, of course, also holds true for therapists with histrionic character traits.

CHAPTER ELEVEN

Abstinence and Actualization

In bipersonal analysis, abstinence has different meanings for the analyst and the analysand. The analyst should not satisfy wishes of his own or wishes of the patient that do not contribute to the therapeutic process. The definition of abstinence in psychoanalysis is mainly determined by factors that refer to the oedipal phase of development. Accordingly, sexual acts between patients and analysts are excluded. On the transference level they would violate the incest taboo. Touching is not normally allowed in psychoanalytic therapy since physical contact can always be experienced on a sexual level. On the other hand, it is permitted to satisfy a patient's narcissistic needs to a certain degree. The analyst is expected to listen attentively to his patient and concentrate on the patient only. This, among other things, gives narcissistic support. The patient's oral needs may be satisfied on a symbolic level. Within limits, the patient may be fed with words, but not in other ways. Freud is reported to have fed at least one of his patients in a concrete way, but this was an exception in the pioneer days of analysis.

The therapist should not try to get narcissistic support from the patient and not have the patient talk with the motive of being fed with words. The therapist should not let the patient know when he is in need of narcissistic support or hungry for material.

The patient's abstinence is of a different kind. He may talk about instinctual wishes, including sexual ones, but he must only talk about them, he or she must not approach the therapist in order to have them fulfilled, this would be considered a violation of the boundaries that confine the analytic setting.

Thus, in the narcissistic realm, patients may expect to be satisfied to a certain degree; in the oral realm satisfaction must be confined to symbolic acts; in the sexual realm satisfaction that transcends talking about sex is forbidden. Male patients do not, as a rule, want to have sex with their female analyst, more often they expect preoedipal satisfaction.

Since no analyst is present in self-analysis, abstinence must be defined in a different way. The self-analysand's wishes cannot be directed towards an analyst. They are usually directed to fantasy objects or to real people outside the self-analytic setting.

In bipersonal analysis the analysand is expected not to make any important decisions without having worked on them in his analysis. In a similar way, the self-analysand could decide not to make any important decisions without having analysed them. However, the rule not to make any important decisions that may alter the course of an analysand's life without having talked about them in analysis stems from a time when analyses were very brief. Also, in Freud's time, many decisions that could be expected to change an analysand's life required a legal act. In the upper middle class, people did not usually sleep with another without being married or at least engaged. In the Western industrialized countries of today, this is no longer so. In reports on an analysis that are published in our time, there often is information about a patient sleeping with a person he or she was not married to without the analyst taking this up as a major decision.

As we all know, decisions can be made by doing nothing. He who refrains from sleeping with a woman he is not married to decides not to do so. This may have an influence on his future life. Avoidance may have consequences that are similar to the consequences of a decision. If we make it a rule that the patient should not make life-important decisions without talking about them in analysis, absurd consequences will follow. The patient may not decide *not* to sleep with a woman without having worked through the alternatives in analysis.

Abstinence in self-analysis could mean that the self-analysand tries some self-analysis before every decision that he thinks might turn out to be important. Some decisions must be made on the spot but others can be postponed without harm being done. Abstinence in self-analysis could result in habitually postponing decisions. Thus abstinence can, like everything, be engaged in the service of resistance. It can provide rationalizations for avoidance. A self-analysand could avoid making a positive decision by considering the pros and cons for so long that the time for making an active decision would have passed. A self-analysand should try to find out whether he has a tendency to postpone decisions and put everything in the service of postponement or whether he has a tendency to act 'spontaneously' without considering the consequences. He could establish rules of abstinence that would take such propensities into account.

A self-analysand who realizes that he has repeatedly engaged in particular kinds of relationships should ask what his part in this has been. In his bipersonal analysis he will usually have become acquainted with some kinds of re-staging of his past. With changing life conditions and with increasing age, new re-stagings may occur that should be recognized as such.

Any first re-staging is difficult to recognize, since there is no recent repetition that could point to re-staging having occurred. Other criteria must be used, such as a feeling of unease when the relationship changes. Intense feelings that are difficult to explain also point to re-staging taking place. These criteria are not very specific. They can only point to the *possibility* of re-staging taking place, they cannot prove it.

Of course, we re-stage past relationships all the time. We look for partners that fit the objects in our inner world. This happens with almost every choice of partner. If a chosen partner does not fit transference in some ways, he is often induced to show a behaviour that does fit. This requires an expense of energy from the person who identifies projectively and from the person who is projectively identified – for instance he or she must suppress their own spontaneous ways of acting in order to conform to the projective identification. Re-stagings often occupy much of our capacity to observe, making us overlook important occurrences in our relational network. Disadvantages may result.

An ambitious man had trained as a social worker and then studied medicine in order to become a psychiatrist. He chose to marry a woman who was an aeronautical engineer's daughter with a college education but without professional training. She expected much of him in the way of a career, wanting him to rise to a leading position in the hospital where he was employed. This position would have involved much administrative work and less work with patients, which he was good at and which he liked. His wife's ambition went parallel with his, derived from his own ambitious disposition, but he would have liked to become a psychiatrist in private practice, so the goals were different. He applied for the position his wife wanted him to obtain and got it, but he was not good at the administrative part of it. Also, he found it difficult to help his juniors in attaining professional competence, while he was excellent at helping people who could never be his equals to develop their capacities. He left the hospital with a sense of failure, divorced his wife and succeeded in private practice.

A person preparing for an exam may look for a person who helps him, reproducing a situation that happened before when a parent helped, and disregard other possibilities, for example the possibility of learning to do the work by him or herself, something which he or she avoids by looking for a helper.

Some people in difficult life situations go to the cinema in order to distract themselves from their everyday problems. A person who re-stages may re-stage his own 'cinema', taking an acting part in what occurs but perhaps neglecting some of his real-life problems.

CHAPTER TWELVE

Being Tolerant and Tactful in Analyzing Oneself

In a bipersonal analysis the analysand learns to be more tolerant in dealing with his Id impulses than he was before. In bipersonal analysis he may have come to learn about some such impulses and he may have become acquainted with them. This makes it easier for him to become acquainted with other impulses of a similar kind.

An analysand in a bipersonal analysis has become acquainted with elements of clinical theory that apply to his or her Id impulses: to those he or she has come to know and to others he or she had no opportunity to become acquainted with because the defence against them could not be made permeable. Clinical theory can also help to deal with the consequences of Id impulses that appear as symptoms.

Some wishes, like the wishes of paedophilia or necrophilia, are judged as bad by almost everybody. Other kinds of impulses many people consider to be admissible or even normal, but may cause great anxiety in some persons. This applies, for example, to homosexual impulses.

Resistance may be motivated by the fear of encountering impulses that are socially unacceptable or that are severely judged by one's superego or ego ideal. In bipersonal analysis many impulses that society does not condone or that the analysand rejected for various reasons will have been explored. These impulses will no longer frighten him. On the other hand, every analysand will have come to know that not all impulses can be reached and worked on in every analysis and at every stage of life (see also Freud 1937). Some impulses are only activated by changing life conditions.

It is not only Id impulses that cause shame. Shame may be caused by the fact that an ego lacks ego functions other people have at their disposal. For example, a person may discover that he or she lacks certain talents and competencies that others have. Shame is especially great if there was prior illusion of having them. Of course, this proves especially traumatic if such competencies and talents are in fact needed for one's professional work. Not everybody is suited for the profession he is interested in. This also applies to psychotherapy. Neurotic traits may enhance interest in psychotherapy but you also need talents. Therapists with restricted diagnostic competencies and a restricted capacity to choose the right way of treatment – as, for example, therapists with schizoid character traits who, as it were, seem to look through the behavioural surface of their patients but whose diagnostic estimates are much distorted by projection – may learn about their lack of competence at a stage of training when it has become difficult to change careers. Some therapists discover it only in private practice. Working in a clinic, they had colleagues and superiors who could compensate their lack of diagnostic and prognostic abilities. After having finished their training, they often go without supervision. This makes their lack of competence become clear. They may then rationalize their deficiencies, for example, they refer to the fact that especially difficult patients are often sent to therapists who have just started in practice. Ubiquitous difficulties are used to explain everything. If a therapist starts doubting his rationalizations, he may arrive at the unpleasant insight that he is unable to do good work in private practice.

Obsessive-compulsive traits are not very popular with psychotherapists, probably because obsessive-compulsive patients may be such a chore. On the other hand, obsessive-compulsive character traits in a therapist can be quite useful in some ways, which helps in rationalizing them.

A character trait viewed with contempt almost everywhere is cowardice, a lack of social courage in times of peace or a lack of physical courage in a war. Cowardly people or people who are supposed to have been cowards in a certain situation must have excellent other traits if they want to compensate for this.

Of course, courage is a complex character trait. It may have something to do with altruism, for example in defending other people against aggression. Changing one's job may call for a courageous decision. Separations from other persons often take courage.

Not making decisions is often rationalized in various ways. Separation can be postponed or not arrived at altogether from a fear of hurting the other person. On the other hand, separations can be accomplished without regard for the partner's interest. Usually, 'good reasons' can be found for either procedure.

Rationalization then can help to stay in harmony with one's ego ideal and superego demands and to defend one's reputation. People who lack tolerance of their own weaknesses and fear the judgement of others will rationalize most.

Tact is an interpersonal phenomenon. At first sight it is difficult to imagine how tact could be used in dealing with oneself. Some people who employ tact in dealing with others can be very aggressive with themselves. The reason is often narcissistic. Such people consider themselves to be better than others, therefore they demand more from themselves than from others. If they cannot fulfil their own demands, they experience narcissistic rage directed against themselves. Narcissistic rage has totalistic properties. The intensity of narcissistic rage does not correspond to its cause in the way other kinds of anger do. The tendency to direct narcissistic anger against oneself makes self-analysis difficult. Practically everybody who has experienced a bipersonal analysis will know the problem if he has it, but it may not have been adequately resolved. A self-analysand who has a problem of narcissistic rage should address this with priority.

Strictly speaking, it is impossible to use tact in dealing with oneself if you define using tact as being careful not to cause injury when imparting information. Since, in self-analysis, it is not possible to consciously retain information from oneself, tact in the usual sense has no meaning, but it is an important factor in bipersonal analysis. However, there is a radical way of disregarding or suppressing one's emotional reactions in self-analysis that may finally lead to an eruption of narcissistic rage or to getting rid of the reactions by projection or by projection combined with displacement. A person analysing his own conflicts and deficiencies should watch out for his emotional reactions to what he discovers and adopt a speed of progress suited to his limits of tolerance. This is a kind of tact that can be used in self-analysis.

CHAPTER THIRTEEN

Working Through

Psychoanalytic case histories in scientific journals that sum up analyses of some years duration contain much information about what happened between patient and analyst and about the reciprocal influences of relationships outside on the analytic dyad and vice versa. Working through is only referred to in passing, if at all, and the reader might ask whether the authors considered working through to be important enough to write about it (and, indeed, do it in analysis). The idea that change can result as a by-product of the psychoanalytic process seems still to be shared by many analysts. There are collusions of omnipotence between therapist and patient; they may also establish a conjoint transference of ideal objects on 'Psychoanalysis'.

Just as research does not just *happen* in analysis, therapeutic change does not just happen in some magic way. Certainly, some experiences in the transference relationship are impressive enough to cause change without working through but this is far from being the rule. Some insights are similar to the light of dawn which would not change into daylight if the earth would stop and remain fixed in space. Insight at first sheds just a little light on the interpersonal and intrapsychic scene, as the light of dawn does. Only the contours are visible, details are lacking and the colours are weak or none are to be seen. This happens in bipersonal analysis and also in self-analysis.

Some analysands learn to transpose their insights on a level of abstraction that will make them appear clearer but less able to exert an influence towards change. Connection with interpersonal detail and with the details of internal conflict are lost. Some insights are like a drawing that gives only the contours. Such drawings may easily change into caricature. The patient's subjectivity, along with a process of abstraction, has resulted in pictures that create strong impressions but are too far away from the real phenomena they are supposed to depict.

Resistance that is stronger than the wish to know is often motivated by a wish to keep what is familiar (König 1982; 1992; 1995a). Putting an insight into practice demands learning new things and 'forgetting' old ones. The learning process by itself would demand work and cost time, without any resistance being active. Anybody who changed his technique in playing a musical instrument or in playing tennis or who tried to learn new turns in skiing and found it difficult to do so, although he was eager to learn the new technique, will understand this, as will people who, working with computers, have changed from one type of software to another.

Often it is easier to learn something entirely new than to modify procedures. So it is often not easy to learn a language that is similar to a language one already knows without producing a mix-up, for example learning Italian after having learned Spanish.

Being able to defend one's position in a quarrel, something a person may want to learn with the help of analysis, may be located on a continuum between letting the other person have his way on one side and being blindly aggressive on the other side. A person who habitually lets his adversaries have their way often finds it easier to act in a blindly aggressive fashion than to take a stand and defend it by arguments. Winning an argument, not just getting something off one's chest, must be learned. Complex social techniques must be acquired, which is often difficult to do within a short period of time. The idea that it would be sufficient to work on resistances (Brenner 1987) in order to achieve complex changes of behaviour is only valid if the required social competencies exist in a person whose symptoms just prevented him or her from employing them. This may happen if psychic symptoms appear in adult life.

Of course, social competencies can atrophy if they are not used for a long time. This is one of the factors that makes treating chronified neuroses so difficult.

CHAPTER FOURTEEN

Concentrating on the Past
as a Resistance

In self-analysis, this is a resistance that can be difficult to overcome. In bipersonal analyses, analyst and analysand may collude in directing too much of their work to the analysand's past, not going back to present object relationships and establishing the appropriate connections. Fixation on the past as a resistance must, however, be differentiated from dealing with past traumatic events, where much working in the past may be necessary.

Also, an analysand who stays bound to his primary family will, of course, think more of his parents than a person who has passed through adolescence into adulthood, gaining a certain distance from the primary family. Fixations in adolescence often occur when adolescents leave home without dissolving the bonds that tie them to their parents.

Adolescents who abruptly separated from their parents for reasons that are external to the primary family or to themselves are usually less bound to their parents than adolescents who separated from home as the result of an interpersonal conflict that transgressed their limits of tolerance. Adolescents who separated from their primary family for external reasons usually project their parental images on persons in the new environment, develop an ambivalent relationship with them and then stage conflicts that permit them to separate in a way that is similar to the way they would have separated from their primary family.

When an adolescent creates a distance from his primary family, his peers become more important. This is also true for adolescents who prematurely separate from their primary family for external reasons. Wishes to have close relationships are directed to people in the peer group. However, if separation was a means to deal with interpersonal conflict, the real parents remain more important. They are experienced in a very ambivalent way. The positive side of the ambivalence is often defended against, while negative feelings occupy the psychic surface. Such an adolescent's longing for good relations with his parents – not with parent substitutes, but with the real parents – may come up only when a parent dies.

Such a fixation on the parents must be treated in a way that is different from the way one should deal with a fixation on the past which helps to avoid dealing with conflicts in the present. Ruminating the past as a resistance may be episodic or habitual. Of course, the habitual thing is more difficult to deal with. Resistive one-sided interest in the past should be treated in the same way as other one-sided interests (Greenson 1967).

Analysis (which holds the past in high esteem) may be misused by such analysands. They deal with the past, often quite freely, but as mentioned above, they resist establishing connections from past to present and vice versa, which is, after all, the ultimate aim in dealing with the past.

A fixation on the primary family often causes the analysand to think much about his parents or siblings and little about people he deals with outside the primary family. As mentioned above, this may be the case when adolescents tear themselves loose from their primary family without dissolving their bonds, but there are less dramatic instances of being fixated on the primary family. Some adolescents experience their parents going into exile inside the family. Such parents have in a way abdicated, they let their adolescent children act as they like, thereby making separation difficult or impossible. In extreme cases family therapy may be necessary. This can even be appropriate after a bipersonal analysis. Although the original, euphoric indications for family therapy have been reduced to a more realistic level, for people who as adolescents have not separated from their family, family therapy may be the treatment of choice.

A self-analysand who had the bad fortune to choose an analyst who likes to dive into the past, avoiding his patient's present problems, can in self-analysis work on what was missed by trying to establish the links that were not established in bipersonal analysis. Therapists with such an analysis often know their parental objects very well by talking about them or perhaps by asking them questions and hopefully by working on their manifestations in transference. They may later use this knowledge to compare them with the people they actually deal with. Luborsky's (1984) concept of the central relational theme can be of help here because it draws attention to the actual object relationships and helps to proceed from the surface into the depth. In this way links that were not established in bipersonal analysis can be established after all. Luborsky's concept consists in finding out what kind of relational wishes a patient has, how objects react to them and how the patient reacts to the object's reaction. Fixations in adolescence are a prime subject for self-analysis of analysts whose bipersonal analysis was conducted at a time when fixations in adolescence were but rarely addressed.

An example: husband and wife are having breakfast. The husband reads a morning newspaper. The wife asks: 'Why don't we talk more with one another?' The husband answers: 'Please, propose a theme'. The wife thinks: 'What an asshole', but says nothing. This little episode, which the wife described in a therapy session, gave not only information about a withdrawn and somewhat naïve husband, but also about the patient who, instead of saying what she wants, poses a question that does not address her emotional needs. When the husband responds on a non-emotional level, asking his wife to propose a theme for discussion, she reacts by silent devaluation. This may derive from the way people acted in the patient's primary family, the patient perhaps identifying with her mother or having had similar experiences as a child wanting to come into emotional contact with her father. By working on the relational episodes, one can find out what is being repeated and what the motives for repeating are, for example the wish to conserve patterns of behaviour that are familiar and thereby continuing to feel safe.

CHAPTER FIFTEEN

Identity Resistances

In our times, norms and values change fast. Male and female roles have changed a lot during the last few decades. This has something to do with the fact that women train for jobs that were formerly held by men. Women feel they have a right to work outside the home and they want to be supported in doing so not only by society at large but also by their partners, whom they ask to take on part of the homework and part of the work connected with the upbringing of children. Women also demand more sexual freedom than they did formerly.

Most women who work outside the home have mothers who did not. These women's mothers cannot serve as models for how to combine the roles of a career woman, a housewife, and a mother. Similarly, many men lack models for being a partner to such a woman, since their fathers had housewives and not career women as partners.

Identifications with parents in the primary family are in conflict with the identities derived from a peer group. In addition, most young professionals do not have parents who went to university. In Germany there is a manifold increase in the number of students. Only a small percentage are children of parents who were students themselves. There is a conflict between identifications with the upper-middle-class peer group and a lower-middle-class or lower-class parental couple. I am myself among the few of my generation whose mother, a paediatrician, worked outside the home. This has saved me from some conflicts I find in my patients.

If a balance between identities has been established or if one identity prevails whilst another identity is suppressed, a state of relative stability has been reached that is often difficult to question (Erikson 1968). In many analyses, matters of identity did not take up much time – perhaps because the analyst was at a loss to deal with them. In such cases the resolution of identity conflicts is left to self-analysis. If these conflicts are held underground, in order not to disturb a precarious balance, they may increase resistance to self-analysis as a whole; self-analysis might uncover them. This is a situation in a way somewhat similar to the analysand having a secret that he must not tell his analyst.

Of course, conflicts between identities pertaining to various social strata, even if they have an influence on conflicts with the primary family, can cover up something else (König 1993; 1995b). As described earlier, a conflict of social identity may cover an oedipal conflict and an oedipal conflict may symbolize a social identity conflict. I think it is important to consider both possibilities. Colleagues from a higher social strata may be experienced as parents who do not want to let a child (a person from a lower social strata) share their life. On the other hand, as we know so well, one's own adolescent children are in many ways a second edition of oedipal conflicts. They may keep a self-analysand from considering his identity conflicts pertaining to adolescence because this could stir up oedipal conflicts he has not entirely resolved. Identity conflicts related to social strata may re-emerge when grown-up children feel ashamed on visiting their parents.

CHAPTER SIXTEEN

Dreams in Self-Analysis

Bipersonal analyses vary greatly as to the extent dreams are used. Also, in professional self experience groups, dreams often do not play a prominent part. This will have an influence on a self-analysis that follows such a group. The analysand plays a large part as to the role dreams will play in his analysis, but the analyst has an influence too. If he shows great interest in dreams, like Freud (1900) did and like Greenson (1967) seems to have done, an analysand will bring more dreams into analysis than if he is under the impression that the analyst does not care very much about them. Of course, having analysed many dreams may be of help in a self-analysis that follows bipersonal analysis.

In some cases a self-analysand may be much more interested in dreams than his training analyst. The training analyst may have divided his attention between several kinds of material and the self-analysand is now free to follow his interest in dreams as much as he likes, and much more than he did in his analysis or in his self experience group.

Self-analysis of dreams is not easy. After all, the dream censor will try to hide latent contents and change them by dream work in a way to make them incomprehensible to the dreamer himself. Nevertheless, analysing dreams is possible and can be useful in self-analysis but I concur with Calder (1980) in that micro symptoms and day-dreams may be even more important.

Associations that seem obvious can be considered unimportant because of their obviousness, but they may nevertheless be important.

The dream censor then works as Edgar Allen Poe described for the 'purloined letter': the letter was lying there for all to see and this was the reason why it was not discovered.

Not all wishes in a dream must first be deduced from the manifest dream by means of free association and interpretation. The manifest dream often contains wishes that could not be experienced during the day since in daytime this was not possible in safety (compare Weiss and Sampson 1986). The security provided by the sleeping state, cutting wishes off from co-ordinated movement, makes it possible for the wish to appear in a manifest dream. In the waking state such wishes are often repressed if the person to whom they are directed is in the room. They may become conscious when this person has left, or not even then, but only in a dream.

Aggressive feelings that were covered up by having sex may remain repressed while the couple are awake and reappear in a dream. Freud (1912) wrote that it is difficult to tell persons about feelings that concern them. It is often difficult to even experience feelings in the presence of such a person. The feelings become manifest in a dream.

There may be several reasons why feelings are suppressed in the presence of the persons to whom they are directed. One reason may be the fear of impulses to act that might be caused by feelings. Another may be fear of one's conscience. Knowing his or her loving feelings can make a person ashamed if they are not reciprocated. Aggressive feelings may cause shame if they are experienced as a loss of control. Also, losing control of one's actions under the influence of emotions can be feared. In realistic anxiety the consequences of one's impulses may be anticipated and cause the anxiety. Being swamped by Id impulses means something different. It means regression to a stage when ego control was not yet developed, as in the stage of an angry infant who moves in an unco-ordinated way, that is in some ways similar to a grown-up person running amok. A grown-up person fears not only the destructive consequences of raw aggression but also helplessness. A person who hits everything and everybody cannot direct his aggressive impulses in order to effectively defend himself. In the manifest dream such impulses may appear more or less undisguised. It is probable that there is more aggression and more sex in today's manifest dreams than in Freud's times because we have become more permissive towards our instinctual impulses and permit ourselves to have day-dreams about them.

This is markedly true for sexual fantasies which in Freud's times were taboo for many people, especially for women from the middle and upper classes, where a double standard of sexual behaviour was prevalent: as in our times, aggressive impulses that were permitted to become conscious if they seemed in some way justified.

Many people permit themselves aggressive fantasies against various people but stop short of putting them into practice. They can often dream quite freely about them.

Defences between the present unconscious (Sandler and Sandler 1983; 1985) and the conscious have become more pragmatic, as it were.

The work of a dream censor is not essentially different from what defences do during the waking state. It is influenced by ego, superego and ego ideal demands. However, in a dream, defence mechanisms are activated that are not usually employed in the waking state – like condensation or representation by the contrary. The present unconscious is connected to the conscious and therefore to information collected about the social conditions a person lives in. It seems to have access to this knowledge during sleep. Thus, during sleep, the present unconscious seems to 'know' that the dreamer's possibilities of co-ordinated motor movement are restricted or practically absent and whether he or she is at present in touch with other persons. This holds true if a person concerned by the dream sleeps in the same bed. It is said to sometimes happen that a husband or wife call out their lover's name when they dream of her or him but this happens but rarely. It would be a sign of the present unconscious not knowing that the partner is present in the same bed.

Various techniques of working with one's dreams seem to be practised. Many analysts recommend to write down one's associations to a dream. I make very little notes when listening to a patient. I do not make notes during a first interview. In therapy I try to use free-floating attention and make some notes afterward. However, in associating with a dream of my own I more or less mechanically write down the ideas it triggers in me, thus preventing myself from too much selection of the 'important information'. The same is true for my associating with a situation where a micro symptom appeared. Interpreting what I wrote down is done as a second step. Calder (1980) also recommends mechanically writing associations down. Associations that are in some way unpleasant are then not so easily left out.

CHAPTER SEVENTEEN

When Does the Therapist Remember Dreams That Have Something to Do With His Patients?

The patient's presence during the hour reduces a therapist's safety. A dream about the patient may open part of the analyst's unconscious that relates to the patient. There is a danger of acting upon impulses that might come up while the therapist thinks about the dream. Linking a dream that concerns the patient to what happens during the hour may be safe if the therapist feels safely lodged in his therapeutic role regarding his manifest behaviour.

For many therapists, remembering a dream in which the patient appears undisguised is cause for alarm. However, such dreams seem to appear quite frequently, as discovered by Lester, Jodoin and Robertson (1989), but they are not an everyday occurrence. A therapist may regard the patient and himself from the vantage point of that dream. The therapist will probably have formed a hypothesis about the meaning of the dream and will probably want to validate or falsify it.

A therapist's dreams where a patient appears disguised may be remembered before, after or even during an hour without the therapist knowing in which way it connects to the patient. There are also cases where a dream is connected to the therapist–patient relationship, but it serves purposes of resistance. The therapist starts thinking about the dream, but to no avail. His attention is deflected from the here and now.

The dream can also have something to do with the person on whom countertransference is displaced, or a dream can appear when the therapist's attention wanders during the hour, and then perhaps attach itself to some important outside relationship in the therapist's life. The therapist wants to concentrate on his work but is prevented from doing so. The dream may draw his attention away from the patient and towards something else that is important for him. Connections with the patient may appear only later.

A therapist was thinking about his son who might take drugs, become dependent on them and be infected with HIV. There had been cases of heroin use at the school his son was attending. The matter had been on his conscious mind for some days. He had had dreams where his son appeared in dangerous situations but was saved at the last moment. There were also dreams in which his son was not saved and got killed. That had something to do with aggression caused by disappointment. He would have liked to have a son he could rely on. Also, troubles his son had caused in former years were restaged in the dream – for example, the son, who was of an adventurous disposition, had hitchhiked to another town where he had been picked up by the police.

The therapist remembered all this in an hour with a patient, who was in no danger of becoming dependent on drugs but was promiscuous and could have been infected with HIV and there had been some question of his breaking off treatment and moving to another town. All this caused the therapist to be afraid of losing the patient, whom he fundamentally liked but who also caused him aggressive feelings which he had suppressed.

CHAPTER EIGHTEEN

Sexuality

There is more to love than just sex. Among other things, love brings narcissistic supply. Freud (1915), in his paper on transference love, mentioned that it may be difficult to resist demands for love by a patient who is selective in her choice of partners. Being loved by a woman who is selective in choosing a lover brings more narcissistic supply than if the woman were promiscuous.

Oedipal fantasies may play an important role. The therapist may imagine himself to be a better partner to the patient than the partner she has or has formerly had. Oedipal fantasies of saving 'mother' from 'father' may be prominent.

Every therapeutic relationship is non-symmetrical. The therapist is in a helping position, which makes him appear strong. This can make a therapist attractive to a patient who would otherwise not find him attractive at all. A therapist concentrates on a patient to an extent that is rare in everyday life. It practically happens only with people who are in love. Compared with the therapist's attitude, the real partner of a patient may appear to neglect her. Of course, there may be conflicts of interests between partners which will not occur between the patient and the analyst, who do not live together, and a therapist will be much more tolerant of a patient's demands. Even if he does not fulfil them, he will not label them as 'infantile' or 'foolish', which the partner might do. Thus the therapist can easily be experienced as a better partner (Rohde-Dachser 1981).

However, if the analyst and his patient were to become partners in an everyday sense, the therapist would change his behaviour and become more similar to the patient's present partner in many ways. There would be conflicts of interest and the therapist would cease to behave in a therapeutic manner. The patient would perhaps realize that she had fallen in love with an illusion created not only by transference but also by the therapist behaving according to the demands of his therapeutic role. The patient would realize that she had mistaken such behaviour for attitudes that would also show up in everyday life.

Transference and counter-transference analysis help to find out why a patient fell in love with the analyst (and why the analyst may have reacted by falling in love himself). Of course, transference and counter-transference analysis, as well as taking the analyst's role into account, will not always explain everything.

We have to keep in mind that transference is a factor in practically all choices of partner. In everyday life outside therapy its influence is smaller than in therapy, but it cannot be excluded that patient and analyst might have fallen in love if they had met on another occasion and it cannot be excluded that a marriage between them would have had a good prognosis. Nevertheless, it would be very difficult to transform love arising in a therapeutic relationship into love that stands the tests of everyday life. A love relationship that started in therapy would thus have a much worse prognosis. This holds true for what the patient would expect and also for the therapist, since love mixed with admiration, as frequently occurs in therapy, would probably evaporate if the patient came to know the analyst as the person he is.

But even if a private relationship with a patient had a good prognosis, the analyst would have to abstain from transforming a therapeutic relationship into a private one because doing this would be detrimental to his functioning as a therapist with his future patients if they knew that he married or had a love affair with a former patient and this would extend to the patients of other analysts who came to know what happened in that case. Safe boundaries are a prerequisite for analytic therapy being possible at all. Patients will repress their loving feelings if they are not sure they can express them in safety. The traumatic consequences of love affairs between analyst and patient that have been reported probably relate to this, the patient feeling abused by a person she confided in (see also König 1995b).

Love affairs between female therapists and male patients seem to be much less frequent than between male therapists and female patients. One of the reasons appears to be that erotic transferences and counter-transferences occur more rarely in male patient/female therapist couples. Many men expect motherly behaviour from a therapist (for the reasons see König 1995b). Female therapists may find a man who is in therapy with her sexually attractive, and feel hurt if the patient does not even consider her as a possible partner. Being a motherly woman in transference is familiar to many therapists, but it loses attraction if a therapist is strictly confined to being the preoedipal mother and is never considered as an adult partner. Women can be afraid of being confined to being 'just' a mother. Other female therapists, to whom a sexual relationship with an adult partner of any kind is problematic, may feel safer in the preoedipal role. Some female analysts thus feel safer in the role of a preoedipal mother. They like to interpret every sexual fantasy from a patient as being a preoedipal wish in disguise. Other female analysts feel that preoedipal wishes are a result of regression caused by conflictual oedipal wishes. However, in daily life there is a mixture of adult sexual, oedipal and preoedipal wishes in almost every couple relationship, the components appearing in different quantities. A female analyst's tendency to reduce everything to one component may make her less effective as a therapist than if she would admit all three.

Being loved means receiving narcissistic supplies to most people. On further reflection a therapist will, however, become aware of the fact that only a small part of the patient's love and admiration would stand the test of reality. He may avoid this kind of reflection if he badly needs narcissistic supplies, for example when he has been narcissistically injured in his private or professional life.

Male therapists want male patients to esteem them because of their 'fatherly competency' and their good-heartedness, real or imagined, and for other things like an analytic competency that shows up in finding the right interpretations and in voicing them at the right time and in an appropriate way. Homosexual involvements between therapists and patients are rare. This may have something to do with the fact that most psychoanalytic societies do not admit homosexual men for training. Things might change if overt homosexuals were admitted more frequently. In training analysis latent homosexual wishes are usually integrated. A man safely anchored in a heterosexual attitude will feel free to deal with homosexual transferences if he has integrated the homosexual aspects of his bisexuality.

In my experience, female therapists tend to completely overlook or only belatedly recognize homosexual transferences in their female patients (König 1995b). It would be interesting to find out whether female analysts who were in analysis with a female training analyst are better at recognizing homosexual transferences because they had experienced them in their own training analysis.

In many countries women find access to the men's world by becoming a man's partner (while men enter it by rites of initiation, like joining the army). In western societies this has changed to a certain degree but the wish to be accepted as a partner and thereby be admitted to the men's world is still active in many women. Thus a female patient falling in love with a male analyst may want to be accepted as an equal partner, which may mean a partner who is equal to a man. That explains the narcissistic injury experienced by many patients whose demands for love are refused by the therapist. They do not see any other possibilities of being accepted as an equal. Such women often rebel against the asymmetry inherent in any therapeutic relationship. They may want a therapist to talk about his own problems in order to establish equality. In classical terminology this has something to do with penis envy, but of course the female patient's demands reflect a wish for equality between the sexes. A male therapist who realizes this may feel that his patient considers the 'male world' to be more attractive than the 'female world' and try to make his patient want to be 'more like a woman' without the wish for equality expressed by 'wanting to be like a man' having been explored.

The best way to deal with sexual wishes of both patient and therapist seems to be a strictly analytic one: analysing what the patient and the analyst really want and at the same time respecting the patient's wishes, even in their infantile aspects, without, of course, fulfilling them. I feel that it is of capital importance to analyse the links between sexual wishes and narcissistic wishes.

CHAPTER NINETEEN

Sado-Masochistic Ways of Relating

Analysts are often criticized for the asymmetrical aspects of the analyst–patient relationship. Of course, all professional therapeutic relationships are more or less asymmetrical but the analytic relationship is probably more so, although it still leaves the patient much leeway (König 1995b). Nevertheless, the asymmetrical aspects of the analytic setting permit the therapist to exert power and have control, which analysts with obsessive-compulsive personality traits may find attractive.

In German the term '*Helferhaltung*' (helping attitude) is often used to describe a propensity to take a powerful helper's position. Some psychotherapists consider this to be common in depressives who like to sacrifice themselves in their work for other people. However, the propensity to sacrifice oneself in helping relationships should rather be called '*Opferhaltung*' or self-sacrificing attitude. A helping attitude is more common in obsessive-compulsives who want the power a helping role entails.

In some candidates for psychoanalytic training there is a slight disposition to sado-masochistic forms of relationship, which must be resolved during training analysis. It is very important for any therapist to know about any sado-masochistic propensities left which, if they have not been analysed, are frequently rationalized, suppressed or defended by reaction formation. Reaction formation is a very questionable way of dealing with sadistic or masochistic traits since reaction formation against sadistic leanings can keep a therapist from confronting his patients when this would be helpful.

Manifest sado-masochistic behaviour is often rationalized, buttressed by ideology or projected onto others, patients included. A therapist who wants power, which often becomes apparent in daydreams, should start by trying to find out whether he wants power as a means to an end or as an end in itself. Of course, people who are in some sort of danger often wish to have more power in order to better deal with the dangerous situation. Just as an army can serve aggressive or defensive purposes, an individual can want power for various reasons. Power can be wanted in order to effect change in one's own or in other people's living conditions. Political ideas cannot be put into practice without power of some sort.

However, power can also be wanted for itself. People who want power as an end in itself feel better if they have power and are able to exert it, without always wanting to accomplish something specific. Some people collect power like others collect money: they are satisfied with feeling they could use it if they wanted to.

People fixated on a sado-masochistic way of relating want power in order to be able to take the sadistic position. Of course, sadism and masochism do not only consist in causing or experiencing pain. Humiliating others and being humiliated is an important component.

Humiliation in connection with sexuality is often sought after in ritualized ways of relating where the humiliated person stages the whole thing and thus remains in control. This especially holds true for rituals staged with prostitutes where the fact that the humiliated person gives the prostitute money makes it clear that he is, after all, in control. Similarly, a person who wants to be in a masochistic position may, in his daily life, manoeuvre himself into a position where he is made to suffer, but he will consciously or unconsciously know that he has staged it. The feeling of being morally superior if humiliated can make a humiliated person feel a better human being than the humiliator, a phenomenon Karen Horney (1936) described as masochistic triumph.

People who desire masochistic relationships are often confined to such ways of relating, which may cause unwanted suffering in the end. Seeing people relate in different ways can make them envious and there is a chance in this: in therapy they can try other ways of relating and, perhaps, come to like them. Sadistic behaviour practised without the other person's consent is often buttressed by ideology, as happens in prisons or concentration camps.

Ritualized sado-masochistic behaviour may be rationalized, for example as education which is all to the educated person's good. This often happens in relationships between teachers and pupils or students or in training programmes.

Ritualizing sado-masochistic behaviour with mutual consent often takes the heat from relations outside the ritualized setting. This applies to both sadistic or masochistic people. For many masochists, provoking others into treating them badly and then suffering pangs of conscience has sadistic aspects. What is called moral masochism is probably best understood as a part of depressive behaviour. Of course, manifest sado-masochistic behaviour is rare in analysts, who must have worked on such problems in the training analysis. However, even then, sado-masochistic wishes not reached by analysis may be activated by certain patients.

CHAPTER TWENTY

Influence of One's Personality Structure on the Capacity to Do Self-Analysis

Personality structure has been variously addressed in this book. I would like to add some more information and try to do a summing-up.

People with narcissistic traits may find it advantageous if they have conducted their own bipersonal analysis very much by themselves, the analyst serving as a self object (Kohut 1971). The analyst is thus experienced as an extension of self for much of the time, only later being experienced as a whole object. Working with an analyst, whom the analysand experiences as a self object, helps to acquire a style of working where the analyst can be substituted by other objects that do not participate in the analytic work, like his room or a garden the analysand looks at through the window of the analyst's consulting room. However, narcissistic analysands who, in later parts of their analysis related to the therapist as a whole person, may still fall back on their former ways of relating. Narcissistically structured people, who have come to experience whole object relationships, often easily fall back on part object relationships. The room where self-analysis is done may then serve as a self object or as a transitional object that, as it were, accompanies the self-analysand's analytic work.

An analysand who came for reanalysis to his former analyst told him that he kept some books in the room where he did self-analysis.

Such books had been on a shelf in the analyst's room where the patient could see them during the hour. During his first analysis he had fleetingly thought about stealing them and transferring them to his room. He refrained from doing this but, after termination, he got copies of the books on the analyst's bookshelf. Some of them were out of print so he had to hunt for them in shops that sold old books. In his self-analysis the patient came to question the whole thing and this was one of the reasons why he returned for reanalysis.

Since the whole object relationships narcissistic people have after a bipersonal analysis are often tenuous but much valued, they may not want to endanger them. For example, they can turn aggression against themselves in order not to endanger the whole object relationship, acting in a way similar to depressives. They run two kinds of danger: regressing to a style of relationship that only allows part objects and not whole objects or turning depressive in order not to lose a valued whole object relationship. Self-analysis should concentrate on this.

People with schizoid personality traits have a tendency to create psychodynamic hypotheses that do not fit a particular person but certain classes of persons, men or women or human beings in general. This shows up in the schizoid therapist's way of dealing with his patients and also in the way he deals with himself in self-analysis. With no analyst to compensate for this, a schizoid therapist may stay on a general, abstract level in dealing with what happens in his life and how he reacts to the events.

On the whole, people with schizoid character traits often find dealing with reality, especially with details that compose it, not very interesting or even boring. They prefer retreating to a realm of abstract thought and symbolic fantasy. They have difficulty making use of other people's reactions to them, as well as of their reactions to others. They usually get along best with people that are similar to themselves, transmitting on the same frequency as it were. In order to get along with another person, they must, in a process of abstraction, get in touch with his or her more general propensities. In this way they can get along with people who are somewhat different from themselves.

Therapists with schizoid personality traits often confine their work to certain kinds of patients, which is possible in a region with many patients and few therapists. If they cannot choose appropriate patients, they use selective perception or denial in order to make the patients fit.

Schizoid therapists will use the same procedure in dealing with feedback in everyday life, finding in it little that is new. The same holds true for feedback from their therapists. Since many people are *fundamentally* similar, and since people with schizoid character traits do not consider the differences to be very relevant, they always seem to treat the same patients. A tendency to exclude certain types of people is usually rationalized and buttressed by some kind of ideology.

People with depressive character traits often feel that the therapeutic relationship is a principal therapeutic factor, although they may have accepted theories that allow for more factors. Since they have no partner in self-analysis, and since they are not able to *make use* of people in the way narcissistic self-analysands do, they often look for a person with whom they can have a relationship that is similar to the relationship they had with the analyst in bipersonal analysis. Of course, this may overtax the people they choose, especially so if these people live close to them, so many contacts are possible. If there are conflicts of interest between the 'analysand' and the 'partner in analysis', the 'partner in analysis' may use information the 'analysand' has given him, mistakenly feeling confident that the 'partner in analysis' would deal with such information in the same neutral way his analyst did. This may lead to severe disappointments and to aggressive impulses that a depressive self-analysand may turn against himself. For example, he may blame himself for having confided in the 'partner in analysis'.

Thus a self-analysand with a depressive character structure experienced a depressive episode when her best friend's husband seemed to hint at something that she had told her friend, asking her to keep silent about it. She felt disappointed and turned the aggression triggered by the disappointment not against her friend but against herself, getting depressed. It then transpired that the friend had not told her husband anything at all, the topic just came up without any connection to what she had been told. The depression lifted. Fortunately, she was able to make use of what had happened, exploring her proclivity to defend against aggression by turning it against the self – a matter that had been addressed in a preceding bipersonal analysis but had not been sufficiently worked through. She seemed to have 'forgotten' about this having been a topic in her analysis.

A phobic person in self-analysis misses the analyst as a directing or guiding object (König 1981) that protects him from dangerous impulses arising within himself. Without such an object he may have difficulty finding ideas in association with a dream, he will just remember more details. This propensity of finding more details instead of new ideas may have been worked on in bipersonal analysis but in most analyses an analysand is not really trained to analyse his own dreams. Some analysts even feel that analysing their own dreams would mean that the analysand was resisting, wanting to exclude the therapist. If the phobic self-analysand succeeds in imagining a person he or she feels to be a directing object, he or she may be able to find new ideas to his or her dreams and, in a general sense, move more freely in analysis. If that is not the case, a person may confine him or herself to what has already been worked on in the bipersonal analysis, applying old insights to new situations. Of course, these old insights may fit, and they probably will, if the conflicts the self-analysand experiences happen to be similar to the ones experienced during bipersonal analysis. Thus some further progress may be made.

A phobic self-analysand is not as convinced of the healing qualities of a relationship as a depressive one. In his or her bipersonal analysis he or she will probably have felt dependent on an object substituting missing older underdeveloped ego functions. For this reason a phobic person does not want people to just listen and be friendly, as a depressive person might. In everyday life he or she may pose specific questions, for example: Did I cover too wide a field in this lecture? Did I talk too softly? What did you not understand? A phobic person is usually willing to learn, within the confines of his or her personality structure. A phobic self-analysand with a successful bipersonal analysis will perhaps continue to look for guiding objects, but he or she will try to learn from them in order to improve his or her own ego functioning.

Self-analysands with obsessive-compulsive character traits have a tendency to ritualize self-analysis, more so than others do. It is important for them to use a formalized setting, sitting in a chair or lying on a couch. An obsessive-compulsive person likes to conduct his or her self-analysis in a systematic way. On encountering a micro symptom, he or she will try all possible explanations. If this does not lead to a conclusive result, he or she may start looking for other explanations and keep looking until he or she feels to have solved the problem. Other, perhaps more important, problems may then remain unanalysed. An obsessive-compulsive person in self-analysis has a tendency to fit micro symptoms that arise in a certain situation to one of the explanations he or she knows. If the explanation does not fit in all respects, he or she may try to 'change' the phenomenon, trying to *make* it fit. If no fitting explanation can be found, an obsessive-compulsive self-analysand may feel very uneasy. In a bipersonal analysis there is always the analyst. The analysand can hope that he or she has the right answer, even if it is not communicated. Obsessive-compulsive self-analysands proceed slowly when they do self-analysis because they feel that there should be another person to accompany them, 'four eyes seeing more than two'. However, an obsessive-compulsive self-analysand may, in his bipersonal analysis, have experienced periods of relative chaos that did not totally submerge him. He or she may have experienced that it was not only possible to get out of this chaos with the help of the analyst, but also under his or her own steam. Then an obsessive-compulsive person will be able to move more freely in self-analysis than would be possible without having had this experience, he or she will be willing to take more risks. This is, by the way, one of the reasons why in doing analysis with an obsessive-compulsive person the analyst should be active in mobilizing conflicts by confronting and interpreting resistances. That not only helps bipersonal analysis to become more productive, it also improves the results of future self-analysis, which can bring further improvement.

An obsessive-compulsive patient had landed himself in prison by physically attacking a police officer who had stopped him for speeding and asked for his driving licence. This was during a time in analysis when aggressive impulses were coming through without impulse control having adapted to them. The patient then attacked his analyst, blaming him for his becoming so aggressive and losing control. The transference aspects of the patient attacking the policeman were interpreted as being based on a father transference and on the displacement of aggressive impulses from the analyst to the policeman. When, after termination of the bipersonal analysis, the patient got into a fight with his boss, he was able to analyse the situation without doing things to the boss that would have made him lose his job or landed him in prison.

A male self-analysand of the hysterical personality type in analysis with a man will, in most cases, have worked on his passive feminine wishes and will have competed with the analyst. This competition may be continued in self-analysis. The self-analysand wants to be a better analyst. This may lead to fruitful competition with productive results. However, as in bipersonal analysis, the hysterical self-analysand has problems with working through. He may still have a tendency to expect 'potent insights' that effect improvement by themselves.

A hysterical man often over-compensates passive-feminine wishes by 'macho' behaviour. He expects to succeed in life by getting women to like and admire him. This fundamental problem is usually attenuated by bipersonal analysis, but in most cases still persists. Competition with men is problematic. On the one hand, the hysterical man feels a need to compete while, on the other hand, he is afraid to do so because competition might reveal his passive-feminine longings. Competing with an absent analyst is less dangerous because the analyst will not be present to watch an eventual defeat and he will not be available as an object of passive-feminine wishes. Also, he will not learn about the self-analysand's weaknesses that come up in the course of self-analysis.

A colleague once told me that in bipersonal analysis he had competed with his analyst in fields where he was indeed more competent, for example in research. After terminating his bipersonal analysis, he observed his analyst giving a competent report on institute matters. He suddenly felt tears coming to his eyes, thinking that he had misjudged his analyst who appeared to be much stronger and more competent than he had thought him to be. He also remembered the gains obtained in his bipersonal analysis. All this was accompanied by a feeling of gratitude and the wish to be near his analyst.

If the hysterical man's analyst was female, he may have learned to impress a woman not only by charm but also by work. He will continue to work in self-analysis, especially on his rivalries with men – which he did not have an opportunity to work on directly with a male therapist. Passive-feminine wishes will be feared less because in identifying with a receptive analyst he may have become acquainted with his own feminine traits, perhaps valuing them more. Analogous results may ensue if the analysand of a male analyst gets to know the male analyst's receptive ways of dealing with the analysand.

During bipersonal analysis of persons with hysterical character traits rivalry with father figures is usually prominent, not only on the level of transference to the analyst but also in dealing with external male objects. If the analyst was a woman, the now self-analysand will perhaps have worked on his competitiveness with father through dealing with external objects, perhaps experiencing the female analyst as somebody who recognizes his skill in dealing with other men. The self-analysand may then continue to work on this and recognize his competencies in identification with the female analyst.

A hysterical female self-analysand will, in a bipersonal analysis, probably have worked on her relationship with father. If the analyst was male, male identification may have become reinforced but she will have talked about her difficulties in relationships with women and possibly have learned to perceive women in a more positive way. She will have had an opportunity to fantasize being a strong father's partner. This fantasy is fostered by the psychoanalytic setting, where the analyst always remains in a stronger position. The analyst will have refused to accede to her sexual demands but will have shown strong interest in her. In bipersonal analysis most female analysands do not directly experience a relationship with a weak man.

Probably this will have happened in relationships outside analysis and may have been worked on, but the hysterical analysand will have kept an inner image of a strong analyst/father against whom other men are measured. Few men will stand up to this comparison since the analyst's role must make him behave in a way that fosters idealization, as described in Chapter 18.

An analysand sought to prevent her loving transference from becoming manifest. When she could no longer deny it, she wondered how on earth she could fall in love with a man so punctilious, indeed pedantic, in matters such as starting and ending the hour on time. She dreamed of the analyst, two inches long, lying under a tree, dying. The tree represented a large phallus and the miniaturized analyst represented her defensive view of him. The big phallus and the small man were brought together during further analysis, the phallus becoming smaller and the man bigger. After termination she fell in love with a man she despised and came back for a few sessions of analysis, telling the analyst that perhaps the man was 'bigger' than she thought, as had been the case with the analyst during her bipersonal analysis, but she did not know for what reason she loved him. It then became clear that the man was punctilious in certain ways and that falling in love with him was a displacement for her analyst as an internal object.

If the analyst is a woman, disappointment with mother has usually been worked through. Since disappointment with mother leads many daughters to expect from father what mother could not give them, the female analysand with hysterical character traits will now expect less from men and get on better with women. However, the identification with a strong woman, the female analyst, may then make her expect more from men, in accordance with improved self-esteem that stems partly from identification with the analyst and partly from becoming more independent of men. The now self-analysand may have difficulties in female–male relationships because she thinks she can 'afford' a stronger man but that man should do what she wants him to do and support her in every way. Self-analysis could concentrate on this.

Male, as well as female, hysterical self-analysands usually take a special interest in problems that are rooted in differences of gender. Preoedipal disappointment in mother and fear of the preoedipal and oedipal mother are still prominent in many female analysands at the end of a long analysis, especially if they had a male analyst. Hysterical men have often not sufficiently worked on their disappointment with the oedipal, and also with the preoedipal, father and on their fear of him. In most hysterical people preoedipal and oedipal problems are closely interlinked. Therapists form no exception.

CHAPTER TWENTY-ONE

Further Thoughts on Self-Analysis and Counter-Transference Analysis

Not all therapies that seem to run smoothly really do so. Greenson (1967) pointed out that every stereotyped behaviour of a patient could be a resistance. Also, counter-transference resistance can cause a therapist to deal with a patient in a stereotyped way. In different phases of a psychoanalytic process different ways of dealing with a patient are necessary. Most therapists adapt quite spontaneously to changes in a patient's behaviour.

If a patient's behaviour remains the same, in spite of insight being accumulated, it is, of course, necessary to ask oneself why the therapeutic process does not advance and what one could contribute to making it move again. The therapist should, however, also ask himself what reasons he might have to ignore changes. For example, progress in therapy may mean that the patient becomes stronger, perhaps too strong for the therapist to bear. Changes may also be for the worse, with the therapist not wanting to notice this or interpreting changes for the worse as improvements.

An example: a therapist in supervision with me refused to see that his patient was increasing his consumption of alcohol, even though this had an effect on the patient's behaviour. The student observed that his patient became more irritable and aggressive with the therapist and also with other people. He interpreted this as a desirable result of analysis: blocked aggressive impulses were being liberated. In fact, however, the patient's irritability could be explained by his increased consumption of alcohol.

Every therapist should find out what it means for him if a patient gets worse or if it turns out that he cannot help a patient much or not at all. Many statistics show that 1/5 to 1/3 of patients are little improved, do not change or get worse. Many therapists feel badly if a patient does not improve as much as they had hoped he would. Of course, it may well be that the patient would have fared better with another therapist – no therapist is best for all patients. On the other hand, there are therapists who find an explanation that has nothing to do with them for every failure. This especially holds true for narcissistic therapists, who cannot bear having failed. Depressive therapists have a strong tendency to blame themselves if a patient does not improve, while a more objective observer would find no fault with them. For self-analysis in connection with one's work, it is important to reflect on how one deals with failure.

CHAPTER TWENTY-TWO

Time-Limited Experiential Groups as a Help in Self-Analysis

In a group, as in bipersonal analysis, participants learn to analyse themselves. They also analyse one another. This is different from bipersonal analysis, where there are no people to be analysed, the therapist usually refusing a patient's attempts to do so, as does a group leader. During bipersonal analysis analysands may try to analyse their partner, colleagues at work or friends and acquaintances. This usually leads to trouble since most people do not want to be analysed without an appropriate contract and outside a therapeutic setting. Members of a group usually want to be helped during group sessions, not only by the group leader but also by other members. Feedbacks and interventions by other group members in a workshop can be put in the service of self-analysis.

Groups are a place where dealing with feedback can be learned. Of course, feedback is not always helpful. It can be distorted by the feedback giver's instinctual wishes or by his defences, by transference, by the externalisation of parts of self or just by a feedback giver's lack of empathy.

Feedback may be sadistic, devaluing or in other ways aggressive. I remember a woman patient who habitually used every weakness a male group member had admitted to attack him. For example, she told a patient who had difficulties in having and keeping an erection that she considered him to be 'flaccid' in his way of dealing with women in the group. The connection was not apparent to her, but when it was pointed out, she realized that she held much contempt for men who could not perform. This made her use of admissions of weakness more understandable and motivated her to find out about the reasons for this. However, things do not always turn out this way. I remember a patient whose devaluation of men was ideologically buttressed and could not be changed within reasonable time. She paralyzed the group, making further work difficult if not impossible. I had to transfer her to individual therapy.

Members of a group learn to differentiate between useful and harmful, correct and incorrect feedback. This is important in self-analysis where it is often necessary to critically judge feedback received from other people, like a partner or a colleague at work.

Group members defend their positions, but also move away from those positions if they prove to be irrational. Members learn to deal with feeling hurt, especially by the feedbacks or by the interpretations of other group members who are not in an expert's position. It is easier for most people to accept a feedback or an interpretation from an expert, but, of course, transference may change this. On the whole, self experience groups are very useful for self-analysis.

Self experience groups that take one year or longer usually last for two hours once a week, or several sessions are held on one weekend each month. In any case, the intervals between sessions are longer than in analysis or in individual psychotherapy. As mentioned above, this may motivate people to do more self-analysis than in individual therapy. Also, the time a group member can use to talk about outside problems is more restricted than in individual therapy. This may also provide the motivation to deal with one's specific problems without direct help from the group. The group, as a system, competes with other systems, the primary or secondary family or a place of work (Garland 1982). Changes are brought about in a competition between systems. Of course, every group member participates in the group process all the time, he or she need not talk and be listened to in order to progress. Group members must adapt what happens in the group to their individual problems, which fosters motivation for self-analysis and thereby helps the acquisition of self-analytic competencies. Groups that take place once a month or so would not be well suited for most patients who suffer from severe symptoms.

In self-analysis, having participated in a group that took place at long intervals may be an advantage. However, the self-analysand should realize that he must, in self-analysis, make do without the *special* kind of feedbacks that are given in a group.

Self experience groups also constitute an experimental space for experimenting with social behaviour, increasing competencies in dealing with people. A group member works in two fields. The group itself is a protected experimental field, but rather restricted in time and also in scope. A member's relational network outside a group is less protected, but usually less limited in time and scope. In self-analysis after a group experience the protected experimental field of the group will be missing.

As in bipersonal analysis, a therapist can foster or block the development of self-analytic competencies in a group. The motives are similar to an analyst's in bipersonal analysis. Obsessive-compulsive therapists usually are not keen on much happening outside the group sessions because what happens there is outside their control. They do not encourage group members to try new things in their relational networks, even if they may, in theory, admit a need for this. Hysterical therapists are often bored by patients who talk about things outside the group. New things should happen in the group, not outside, and they want to participate in what happens. What happens outside the group has little interest for them. Such an attitude prevents group members from relating their successes and failures in applying what they have experienced and learned in the group and working on the difficulties that occurred when they tried to do this.

Therapists with schizoid character traits try to make the group members work in harmony with one another. They want people to understand each other, they want to understand people and they want to be understood, all this in the here and now. What happens outside the group is best ignored. Of course, this attitude will also reduce the possibilities of transfer.

Therapists with depressive character traits will try to make people like or love each other. Conflicts are perceived as more dangerous than they are. Outside the group there is a hostile world where people do not love one another. The group can then degenerate into what Battegay (1979) called an 'emotions club' (*Emotionsklub*). People can experience in the group what they cannot experience in any other place. Of course, this also does not foster transfer.

Therapists with narcissistic character traits have a tendency to fantasize members as extensions of themselves. Group members should make much progress, inside and outside the sessions. Such a therapist may feel narcissistically hurt if group members talk about their failures, which also makes transfer more difficult.

Therapists with phobic character traits may fear that group members will fail in everything they do outside the group. They want group members to talk about things they do outside the group in order to extend the group's and the therapist's scope of help. They make group members feel that outside the influence of the group bad things may happen. On the other hand, counterphobic therapists may expect more courage from group members than they can muster and such therapists have a tendency to leave members to themselves. When group members fail to make a counterphobic therapist's expectations come true they may be viewed with contempt.

Summing up, I would say that every personality structure can block transfer and thus decrease opportunities of applying new insights on one's own. This also decreases self-analytic competencies. Some group leaders seem to feel that outside the group nothing good can happen. This reminds me of a saying ascribed to students of Göttingen University in the nineteenth century: '*Extra Gotingam non est vita. Si est vita, non est ita*' (Outside Göttingen there is no life, and if there is any, it is not the same as here). You only need to substitute the word 'group' for the word 'Göttingen'.

CHAPTER TWENTY-THREE

More About the Limits and Possibilities of Self-Analysis

In self-analysis it is easier to overlook resistances than in bipersonal analysis; in bipolar analysis the analyst can help. He can confront resistances a self-analysand will overlook or rationalize.

A problem shared by both self-analysis and bipersonal analysis is that external reality poses limits to change. An older self-analysand may feel self-analysis is not productive enough, but his age would limit changes in bipersonal analysis too. What cannot be changed is often disregarded, in order to avoid confrontation with conflicts between wishes and reality.

However, age is not only a disadvantage. An older person usually knows that he or she has not much time left to change. Old people cannot lightly postpone change, as younger people might do.

Some older people are more free to change than they were in former years. Their children have left home, leaving the parents more independent and freer to move geographically and also in a figurative sense. At the end of a bipersonal analysis young people often mourn the enjoyments of life lost up to now, because of restrictions by neurotically-based conflicts and neurotic symptoms, but they have time left to live in a different way. Some over-estimate the length of time left.

Old people, who know that death is approaching, will feel that little time is left. This may motivate them to really work in self-analysis. On the other hand, older people may think that self-analysis could make them realize that their whole life has been a failure.

Self-analysis rarely brings revolutionary insights. Many self-analyses just amplify what was gained in bipersonal analysis using an experiential group. Confrontations with a 'failed' life can come from the outside, for example if something that has justified a person's existence is lost. Children may die, a business may fail or progress in research achieved by a scientist may prove to be less important than it appeared to be.

Even for people who experience this kind of confrontation, self-analysis may have its advantages. It may help to realize the good a self-analysand has done in dealing with his or her children and with people who in some way worked with them or whom they helped to enjoy life.

Psychoanalysis and psychotherapy will evolve and, hopefully, progress. It might be a good idea to ask, in retrospect, which new developments played no part in one's own bipersonal analysis. In the 1970s and 1980s oedipal conflicts were neglected by many analysts, who turned their attention to preoedipal pathology. Now, the pendulum seems to be swinging back.

The importance of adolescence in the analysis of adults was widely neglected but has begun to be recognized during the past ten years or so (e.g. Erdheim 1983; 1984; 1988; 1993; König 1995a; 1992; 1993; 1995b). In the 1990s the consequences of fixation in a dyadic way of relating have begun to be recognized. This way of relating does not only occur in patients with preoedipal pathology (Abelin 1971; 1975; Ermann 1985; König 1992; Rotmann 1978; 1985).

CHAPTER TWENTY-FOUR

Self-Analysis and the Institute

Most psychoanalysts or psychotherapists, after having finished their own training, become members of a training institution. In business meetings of the institute new members have an opportunity to see their teachers in a different role. Many teaching and supervising analysts know quite well that their trainees are interested in how they 'really' live. This has an influence on their everyday behaviour in lectures or seminars. In a business meeting they usually behave more freely. They fight for their personal interests, sometimes quarrelling about small things. They show narcissistic hurts and disappointments. Business meetings of more than 15 members can be considered as medium groups; business meetings with 30 or more members work as large groups. A large group must be conducted in a very structured way if regressive phenomena are to be avoided. When such phenomena occur, defence mechanisms become prominent, like projection or displacement – often displacement on very small issues. Thus it may happen that the members of an institute fight for hours about a small raise in their financial contributions to the institute, corresponding to a fraction of what they earn in an hour of therapy.

New members may experience this as irrational, and of course they are right. Many colleagues seem to experience some kind of shock on their first participation in such a business meeting. They had idealized psychoanalysis and its proponents and are now shocked by what they observe.

There has been much discussion about the idealization of training analysts. Greenson (1967) felt that in training analysis aggressive parts of ambivalence are often displaced on other members of the institute, for example on seminar leaders or supervisors.

In my country, during the Kohutian period, many oedipal neuroses were diagnosed as narcissistic. Kernberg's writings and lectures increased interest in narcissistic pathology. His recommendation to analyse idealizing fantasies for their aggressive underpinnings seems to have had a salutary effect. Most analyses now have more chances to reach oedipal pathology.

An institution where there is a hierarchy must trigger oedipal transferences. In principle, all full members of an institute have equal rights, but a hierarchy does exist. It is not always the hierarchy between members and their elected representatives that is important.

Something else has more consequence: the difference between members who become training analysts and members who do not. In small institutes all members participate in training in some way, but in large institutes there are more members than will be needed for this. Members who are not very interested in teaching do not participate in training and some members who would like to participate are not admitted – even those who do not really want to participate feel a lack of prestige, compared to those who do. Splits of institutes have had much to do with this.

Self-analysis can certainly help to tolerate disillusionment. It can also help to tolerate narcissistic injuries that probably will occur in any institute.

Disillusionment that concerns one's own training analyst may have consequences for self-analysis because the internal image of one's training analyst plays an important in self-analytic work. In Chapter One I pointed out that a self-analysand may continue an internal dialogue with the analyst which he began during the bipersonal analysis. If disillusionment after termination is experienced as traumatic, such dialogues cannot be continued as if nothing had happened. Disillusionment with one's own analyst can lead to self-analysis being interrupted or terminated for good, and this in a time of transition from training to independent work where a young colleague could well do with self-analytic help. Some young analysts form peer groups and participate in mutual supervision. In talking about their training analysts they may learn that disillusionment about the same analyst concerns different aspects of his personality. That makes the subjective factor in all this clearer.

Seeing an analyst in a different situation does not always increase the objectivity of the image one forms of him. Transferences persist and this makes for selective attention.

Rumours prevail at most institutions, psychoanalytic institutes are no exception. Since members do not meet daily, a rumour will perhaps pass several heads before it can be reduced to reality. This is different in institutions where people meet every day or at least once a week. The fact that the members of a psychoanalytic institute rarely meet makes business meetings more important than, say, weekly or even daily meetings in a hospital or institution dedicated to research.

Former trainee analysands may fear that their training analyst could use his knowledge in institutional politics, also that he could directly impart his knowledge to others – as happened as a matter of course in institutes with a reporting system. Since criteria for advance in an institute are often quite unclear, personal sympathies and aversions may have a large influence on decisions concerned with advancement.

References

Abelin, E.L. (1971) 'The role of the father in the separation-individuation process.' In J.B. McDevitt and C.F. Settlage (eds) *Separation-Individuation* New York: International Universities Press.

Abelin, E.L. (1975) 'Some further observations and comments on the early role of the father.' *International Journal of Psycho-Analysis*, 56, 293-302.

Battegay, R. (1979) *Der Mensch in der Gruppe (People in Groups)*. Bern: Huber.

Brenner, C. (1977) 'Working alliance, therapeutic alliance and transference.' *Journal of the American Psychoanalytic Association (Suppl.)*, 37, 137-157.

Brenner, C. (1987) 'Working through: 1914–1984.' *The Psychoanalytic Quarterly*, 56, 88-108.

Calder, K.T. (1980) 'An analyst's self-analysis.' *Journal of the American Psychoanalytic Association*, 28, 5-20.

Erdheim, M. (1983) 'Adoleszenz zwischen Familie und Kultur' (Adolescence between family and culture). In M. Erdheim *Psychoanalyse und Unbewußtheit in der Kultur (Psycho-analysis and the unconscious in culture)*. Frankfurt: Suhrkamp.

Erdheim, M. (1984) *Die gesellschaftliche Produktion von Unbewußtheit (The Creation of Unconsciousness by Society)*. Frankfurt: Suhrkamp.

Erdheim, M. (1988) 'Psychoanalytische Jugendforschung' (Psychoanalytic research on youth). In M. Erdheim *Psychoanalyse und Unbewußtheit in der Kultur (Psychoanalysis and Unconsciousness in Culture)*. Frankfurt: Suhrkamp.

Erdheim, M. (1993) 'Psychoanalyse, Adoleszenz und Nachträglichkeit' (Psychoanalysis, adolescence and deferred action). *Psyche*, 47, 934-950.

Erikson, E.H. (1968) *Youth and Crisis*. New York: Norton.

Ermann, M. (1985) 'Die Fixierung in der frühen Triangulierung' (Fixation in early triangulation). *Forum der Psychoanalyse 1*, 93–110.

Freud, S. (1900) 'The interpretation of dreams.' In J. Strachey (ed) *The Standard Edition of the Complete Psychological Works of Sigmund Freud (Vols. 4 and 5)*. London: Hogarth Press.

Freud, S. (1912) 'The dynamics of transference.' In J.Strachey (ed) *The Standard Edition of the Complete Psychological Works of Sigmund Freud (Vol. 12)*. London: Hogarth Press.

Freud, S. (1915) 'Observations on transference-love.' In J. Strachey (ed) *The Standard Edition of the Complete Psychological Works of Sigmund Freud (Vol. 12)*. London: Hogarth Press.

Freud, S. (1937) 'Analysis terminable and interminable.' In J. Strachey (ed) *The Standard Edition of the Complete Psychological Works of Sigmund Freud (Vol. 23)*. London: Hogarth Press.

Garland, C. (1982) 'Group analysis: Taking the non-problem seriously.' *Group Analysis*, 15, 4-14.

Greenson, R.R. (1967) *The Practice and Technique of Psychoanalysis*. New York: International Universities Press.

Habermas, J. (1975) *Erkenntnis und Interesse (Individuals and the Acquisition of Knowledge)*. Frankfurt: Suhrkamp.

Horney, K. (1936) 'The problem of the negative therapeutic reaction.' *Psychoanalytic Quarterly*, 5, 29-44.

Junker, H. (1993) *Nachanalyse. Ein Autobiographisches Fragment (Additional Analysis. An Autobiographical Fragment)*. Tübingen: Edition Diskord.

Kohut, H. (1971) *The Analysis of the Self*. New York: International Universities Press.

König, K. (1974) 'Arbeitsbeziehung in der Gruppenpsychotherapie – Konzept und Technik' (Working relationships in group psychotherapy. A concept and its technical applications). *Gruppenpsychotherapie und Gruppendynamik, 8*, 152-166.

König, K. (1979) 'Arbeitsbeziehungen in analytischen Gruppen' (Working relationships in analytic groups). In A. Heigl-Evers und U. Streeck (Hrsg) *Lewin und die Folgen. Die Psychologie des 20. Jahrhunderts (Lewin and the Consequences. Psychology in the 20th century)*. Zürich: Kindler.

König, K. (1981) *Angst und Persönlichkeit. Das Konzept vom Steuernden Objekt und seine Anwendungen (Anxiety and Personality. The Concept of an Internal Guiding Object and its Applications)*. Göttingen: Vandenhoeck & Ruprecht.

König, K. (1982) 'Der interaktionelle Anteil der Übertragung in Einzelanalyse und analytischer Gruppentherapie' (The interactional component of transference in individual and group psychotherapy). *Gruppenpsychotherapie und Gruppendynamik*, 10, 220-232.

König, K. (1992) *Kleine Psychoanalytische Charakterkunde (An Introduction to the Psychoanalytic Study of Character)*. Göttingen: Vandenhoeck & Ruprecht.

König, K. (1993) *Einzeltherapie Außerhalb des Klassischen Settings (Individual Therapy outside the Classical Setting)*. Göttingen: Vandenhoeck & Ruprecht.

König, K. (1995a) *The Practice of Psychoanalytic Therapy*. Northvale NJ: Jason Aronson.

König, K. (1995b) *Countertransference Analysis*. Northvale NJ: Jason Aronson.

König, K. and Kreische, R. (1991) *Psychotherapeuten und Paare. Was Psychotherapeuten über Paarbeziehungen wissen sollten (Psychotherapists and Couples. What Psychotherapists Should Know About Couple Relationships)* Göttingen: Vandenhoeck & Ruprecht.

König, K. and Lindner, W.-V. (1994) *Psychoanalytic Group Psychotherapy*. Northvale NJ: Jason Aronson.

Körner, J. (1989) 'Kritik der "therapeutischen Ich-Spaltung"' (A critique of the concept of a therapeutic split in the ego). *Psyche,* 43, 385-396.

Lester, E.P., Jodoin, R.-M. and Robertson, B.M. (1989) 'Countertransference dreams reconsidered: a survey.' *International Review of Psycho-Analysis,* 16, 305-314.

Luborsky, L. (1984) *Principles of Psychoanalytic Psychotherapy*. New York: Basic Books.

Rotmann, M. (1978) 'Die Bedeutung des Vaters in der "Wiederannäherungs-Phase"' (The importance of father during the 'rapprochent phase'). *Psyche,* 32, 1105-1147.

Rotmann, M. (1985) 'Frühe Triangulierung und Vaterbeziehung' (Early triangulation and the relationship with father). *Forum der Psychoanalyse,* 1, 308-317.

Rohde-Dachser, C. (1981) 'Dyade als Illusion?' (The dyad as an illusion?) *Zeitschrift für Psychosomatische Medizin und Psychoanalyse,* 27, 318-337.

Sandler, J. and Freud, A. (1985) *The Analysis of Defense: The Ego and the Mechanisms of Defense Revisited*. New York: International Universities Press.

Sandler, J. and Sandler, A.-M. (1983) 'The "second censorship", the "three box model" and some technical implications.' *International Journal of Psycho-Analysis* 64, 413–425.

Sandler, J. and Sandler, A.-M. (1985) 'Vergangenheits-Unbewußtes, Gegenwarts-Unbewußtes und die Deutungen der Übertragung' (The infantile unconscious, the present unconscious and the interpretation of transference). *Psyche 39,* 800–829.

Sterba, R.F. (1934) 'The fate of the ego in the analytic therapy.' *International Journal of Psycho-Analysis,* 15, 117-126.

Weiss, J., Sampson, H. and The Mount Zion Psychotherapy Research Group (1986) *The Psychoanalytic Process*. New York/London: The Guilford Press.

Subject Index

Author Index